Introduction

Look in any handbook on vanished rural crafts – in any village history or any coffee table book about the countryside of days gone by – all of them will emphasise the pivotal role once played by the country blacksmith.

Take, for example, Shire Album 24 *The Village Blacksmith*: "The blacksmith's part in the daily needs of village life was vital. He was highly skilled in farriery and he made and repaired tools and equipment for local farms and households." Not only that. According to *The Shell Book of Country Crafts*, he might also make "gates of all sizes, together with railings, balconies, chimney cranes, spits, fire-irons and irons, brackets and hinges." And, according to Ronald Webber, in yet another book entitled *The Village Blacksmith*, he might at times be called on to perform the role of "wheelwright, carpenter, tinker, veterinary surgeon, doctor, dentist, sportsman and many other things."

All these accounts, however, share the same sense of pathos. For as Ronald Webber points out:

"The village blacksmith as a worker in iron and a shoer of horses with his own 'shop' in the centre of a village has almost gone. The place that was once filled with the noise of horses and hammering and with the acrid smell of burning hoofs, and was the gossip mart of the area, has fallen before the onslaught of the motor age... Some blacksmiths' shops have become garages, others workshops for artistic ironwork, but most have gone altogether, with a house name like *The Old Forge* the only reminder that here once was a thriving business."

My grandfather, Walter Murphy, was a player in this story. He was for many years the blacksmith in the Hampshire village of Preston Candover, and throughout the 1950s my brother John and I would spend our school holidays at the Forge Cottage. Grandad was as old as the century and by then was a man of medium build with thick greying hair, huge fire-scarred hands and a rich Hampshire accent. The smithy stood at the end of a yard behind the cottage and there we would often watch him fashioning some piece of ironwork on the anvil. Sometimes we would go with him in his van to visit the stables or inspect a job at a local farm. Occasionally he might allow us to lend him a hand – perhaps pull on the handle of the old iron cutter or turn the enormous grindstone that stood in the meadow behind the smithy.

We never doubted that we had ideal grandparents. But whereas Gran was especially kind, patient and very indulgent, Grandad was a mass of contradictions. He could be both self-centred and generous, cantankerous and obliging. He could fuss over us like an old hen or be as carefree as a summer's morn-

ing. He could be maddeningly slow and ponderous, or enormously funny and entertaining – especially with all his anecdotes of life in Preston Candover past and present.

He spent his working life in a heavy manual occupation, yet his constitution was surprisingly frail. He had a deep love for the countryside, yet he could adorn the meadow with the most ramshackle of galvanised iron sheds and chicken houses. He was a loyal Conservative voter all his life, yet the very word "gentry" could turn him into the most rabid Bolshevik. He liked to give the impression that he was a man whom nobody could cross lightly, yet whenever he was actually crossed, his anger always spent itself harmlessly within the confines of the family home. He was, in short, a "character".

During the 1960s, as John and I progressed to university, we were faced with having to find suitable topics for project work, and it was to meet this need that we first began delving into the history of Preston Candover. Grandad was extremely helpful to us in our research, not only for his memories of village life but also for the many contacts he had in the locality. We did not, however, fully appreciate the depth of his knowledge and experience until 1968 when he was "discovered" by the local press. The newspaper features which subsequently appeared about him brought home to us just what a fascinating story he had to tell. For not only had he begun his career at a time when society was still largely dependent on horse-drawn transport. He had also witnessed at first hand all the changes wrought to the blacksmith's craft by the social, economic and technological developments of the 20th century.

I immediately took steps to ensure this knowledge was preserved by undertaking a series of taped conversations with him about his life, and also by collecting together all the photographs and other memorabilia which had previously lain in drawers and cupboards about the cottage. In due course I also took charge of all the "books" of the business – a stack of ledgers and diaries kept on the dresser in the back bedroom, which could potentially provide a detailed record of the business since the early 1900s.

This book thus tells the story of Walter Murphy's life and times by drawing on both the oral record and the business accounts. In so doing, it provides a case study of the role performed by the country blacksmith in the 20th century and shows in detail how that role fell "before the onslaught of the motor age."

The well-being of a small business such as a village smithy was very dependent on the type of customer who happened to live within the catchment area – their relative affluence, their personal preferences, their particular approach to the running of their farm holding or business. The book, therefore, includes biographical sketches of the smithy's principal customers, so that such considerations can be taken into account.

A particular difficulty arises in the use of names. Grandad was christened Walter George William Redvers Murphy but, once past his childhood years, he was rarely referred to as "Walter". In his early twenties he was nicknamed "Patrick", a name apparently bestowed on any young man with the surname "Murphy". For most of his adult life he was referred to as "Murph", even by his wife. At various stages he was also referred to as "Father", "Dad" or "Grandad". In the text, however, I have referred to him throughout as Walter, even though he himself would have thought this very strange. Also, since I want him to be the central figure in the story, I have referred to myself in the third person.

In regard to terminology, I have followed the approach adopted by Ronald Webber and have used the term "blacksmith" in most instances to stand for "farrier" as well. According to the *Oxford English Dictionary*, a "blacksmith" is "a smith who works in iron or blackmetal", while a "farrier" is a "shoeing smith". However, the village blacksmith was generally both a smith and a farrier. Also, as regards the premises where the blacksmith worked, the terms "smithy", "forge" and "blacksmith's shop" are often used interchangeably – Grandad always referred to his premises as the "shop". In this book I have used the term "smithy" when referring to the premises. The term "forge" I have used only in respect of the hearth on which the iron was worked.

Although this study has been compiled primarily from the business records of the Preston Candover smithy, these have been supplemented where possible by items in newspapers and journals and from a variety of other sources. In this regard I would particularly like to acknowledge the generous assistance I have received from the staff at the Hampshire County Record Office and especially from the Senior Archivist, Sarah Lewin. I would also like to extend my thanks to Ewan Maidment, Executive Officer at the Pacific Manuscripts Bureau, Australian National University.

I am also greatly indebted to a number of people who have advised me on the technical aspects of the blacksmith's craft, or who have supplied me with information or photographs. They include: Mr Mark Andreae, Mr Peter Andreae, Mr Anthony Aris, Mr Paul Bliss, Mrs Angela Brown, Mr Roger Burton, Mrs Joan Clark, Mrs Jan Cole, Mr James Courage, Mr Michael Courage, Mr Charles Crichton, Mrs Gillian Evans, Dr Bridget Drew, Mr John Drew, Captain David Freeman, Mrs Anne Hughes, Mr Edward Jackson, Mrs Jean Kelly, Mr James Kenward, Mr Jeffrey Lax, Mrs Sue Marriott, Mrs Mary Matthews, Mr Ron Messenger, Miss Barbara Nobbs, Mr John Nobbs, Mr Roger Palmer, Mr Barry Parker, Mr George Paul, Mr Ian Paul, Mrs Lucinda Phillips, Mr Edward Roberts, Professor Brian Rowe, Mrs Connie Rowe, Dr John Sheail, Mrs Laurie Sheail, Mrs Melinda Simpson, Mrs Joan Smith, Mr Edgar Stern, Mrs Connie Taylor, Mrs Pamela van Moppes, and Mr Thomas Whitman – plus all those patient and informative people I have encountered at various heavy horse shows and steam fairs over the years.

Finally I would like to thank my son Christopher for his technical assistance in setting out this book, and my wife Janet for her interest and encouragement.

Philip Sheail
April 2007

PHOTOGRAPH ACKNOWLEDGEMENTS

All photographs the property of the author except for those itemised below (photograph number in brackets).

Photographs obtained from photographic libraries, newspapers, journals, and organisations:
   Hampshire Record Office: Series HRO 45M86/5: 37 (14), 96 (16), 116 (24), 62 (28), 69 (30), 101 (31), 94 (34), 78 (38), 71 (49), 177 (50), 68 (74); Series HRO 45M86/42: 28a (20), 19a (85); Series HPP5: 4/50 (7), 2/37 (25)
   Museum of English Rural Life, The University of Reading: 35/33066 (104), 35/15829 (105), (106, 138), 35/7705 (139), (140)
   Illustrated London News Picture Library (101, 102); *Hants & Berks Gazette* 30 October 1959 (146); *Poultry World* 3 July 1936 (82); Royal Thames Yacht Club (129)

Photographs obtained from private individuals:
   Mr M. Andreae (112, 130); Mr A. Aris (73, 76-78); Mr R. Burton (81); Mrs J. Clark (1, 23, 32, 33, 58, 60, 75, 79, 83, 93, 94); Mr J. Courage (122); Mrs G. Evans (136); Mrs J. Kelly (3); Mr J. Kenward (48); Mrs S. Marriott (132); Mrs M. Matthews (97); Mr R. Messenger (56); Miss B. Nobbs (39, 52-55, 61, 65, 80, 96, 98, 99); Mr L. Podmore (Introduction, 150); Mr E. Roberts (100); Professor B. Rowe (67); Mrs J. Smith (62, 109, 137); Mrs P. van Moppes (88, 89, 131); Mr T. Whitman (18).

Newspaper cuttings on page 75 reproduced by courtesy of the *Basingstoke Gazette*, *Hampshire Chronicle* and *Southern Daily Echo*.

Edwardian Times

In his later years Walter Murphy liked to present himself as a bluff good-humoured countryman, living out the life to which he had been born and bred amidst the Hampshire downs. His origins, however, were rather less straightforward than people imagined. In fact, but for the strange workings of fate, he would have grown up to be a thorough-going Cockney sparrow.

His Hampshire roots lay on his mother's side of the family. She belonged to the Padwicks and she came from that part of the county known as the Candover Valley.

The valley lay at the centre of a triangle formed by the towns of Basingstoke, Winchester and Alton. At its bottom end stood the little town of New Alresford where its stream, the Candover Brook, joined the River Itchen. From New Alresford the valley stretched away northwards into the downs for some 10 miles before it became lost amidst the high downland just south of Basingstoke.

This map identifies the towns and villages in the Candover Valley area in the mid-1930s, following changes to the parish boundaries brought about by the County of Southampton Review Order of 1932. One consequence of this Order was the amalgamation of Brown and Chilton Candover into a new civil parish called Candovers. In the case of Wootton St Lawrence and Itchen Stoke, the respective northern and southern extremities of those parishes have not been shown. The thicker boundary lines show which local authority areas fall within the "Adjacent Parishes" and the "Other Local Parishes, etc" (see Graph 2).
Al – *Alton*; An – *Andover*; B – *Basingstoke*; S – *Southampton*;
W - *Winchester*

Above – The village street at Preston Candover in 1902, looking south towards the church with the Post Office and general store on the left. The children are possibly waiting for the Vicar's daughter, Emily Wilson, to pass by on her way to the church for her wedding to James Anderson. (1)

Views of the Candover Valley. Above – Looking north from Preston Candover towards the Crown Inn at Axford and the high down of Nutley and Farleigh Wallop. (2) Left – The Candover Brook at Northington. (3)

A string of villages lay along the valley floor – Old Alresford, Swarraton, Northington and the three Candovers – Brown, Chilton and Preston. The springs of the Candover Brook normally rose in the neighbourhood of Chilton and Preston Candover. Beyond Preston, away to the north and east, the valley became narrower and was joined by a number of tributaries, all of them dry. Amidst these valleys lay the villages of Nutley, Ellisfield, Bradley, Upper and Lower Wield, and Herriard.

Between the settlements the landscape was one of gently rolling farmland, interlaced with thick hedgerows, and dotted with dells and coppices. Meadowland occupied the lower stretches along the banks of the Candover Brook. The ridge tops were covered by a sour clay and here the land was often given over to woodland.

The Padwicks lived at the bottom end of the valley. Walter's grandfather, William Padwick, had started out as a thatcher and farm labourer. Then in 1862 he married a servant girl, Ann Bennett, and thereafter they dwelt at Old Alresford where Ann ran the Post Office and William delivered the mail. They had six children – William, Catherine, Emily, Nell, Bess and Dick.

Catherine, born in 1868, went into domestic service. She started off as a general servant in the home of a tailor in New Alresford. From there she moved to Hertfordshire where she worked as a kitchenmaid in a large house called Leahoe just outside the town of Hertford. Not far from the house stood an establishment called Horns Mill which produced linseed oil. The manager of the mill was George Murphy and at some stage Catherine became acquainted with his son Walter.

The Murphys' Irish roots lay some two generations back with one Michael Murphy who seems to have come to England in the early 19th century and settled down at Louth in Lincolnshire. There he married a local girl and raised a family of some four children. He died in the 1840s, leaving the family in a destitute state. His son George left Louth in the early 1850s and headed down to London, where he eventually ended up in Hammersmith working in an oil-seed pressing mill. In 1856 he married a servant girl, Sarah Ann Jones, and over the next few years he progressed to become the manager of oil mills at Arundel in Sussex and Newton in Lancashire. During that time he and Sarah produced a family of four boys and four girls. Walter was the youngest of the boys, born in Arundel in 1866.

George became manager of Horns Mill at Hertford during the 1870s. The two oldest boys joined him in the mill while the other two were apprenticed to trades in the town. Walter's chosen trade was that of baker and it may have been while delivering bread to Leahoe that he first became acquainted with the young kitchenmaid from Hampshire. They were eventually married in London in June 1896 at the Catholic church of Our Lady of Victories on Ken-

Walter Murphy Senior with his daughter Kathleen in 1899. (4)

4

*Right – William and Katherine Padwick in 1908. (5)
Far right – William Padwick and his nephew Walter Murphy outside the Forge Cottage in about 1903. (6)*

sington High Street. By this time George had given up managing Horns Mill and the family had dispersed, mostly to London.

Walter gave up the bakery business and became a carman for Idris & Co., mineral water manufacturers, based in Camden Town. On Saturday 21 July 1900 he went out on a delivery across the river towards Blackheath. He was driving a three-horse van and was accompanied by a youth in charge of a one-horse van. Round about midnight they stopped at the top of a hill in Lee Road, Lewisham, where the youth parked his van at the edge of the road. He then climbed up next to Walter and they proceeded on their way down the hill. On reaching the bottom they suddenly realised the other van had slipped its skids and was now hurtling down the hill towards them, pushing the terrified horse before it. Walter at once jumped down from his van but, as he went to grab the horse's reins, he slipped and fell. The van wheel went over his head, killing him instantly.

The accident left Catherine with a girl of two named Kathleen and another baby expected later in the year. So, once Walter had been buried at the Finchley Cemetery, she headed back to the family home at Old Alresford. There the baby was born on 15 November 1900 – a boy whom she named Walter George William Redvers Murphy. He was named Walter after his father, George and William after his grandparents, and Redvers after General Sir Redvers Buller. Clearly the South African War was a matter of some moment in the Padwick household.

As a widow in her early thirties, Catherine had little option but to return to domestic service. And so in the early summer of 1901 the Padwicks came together at Old Alresford and there Catherine asked her siblings if they would take care of the children. As a result of these deliberations, Kathleen was to spend her childhood years at Bournemouth. Little Wally meanwhile was to be adopted by his uncle, William Padwick, and it was through this decision that he now came to live in the village of Preston Candover.

*

Born in 1865, William Padwick had been apprenticed in his teens to the Old Alresford blacksmith, William Rampton. The business encompassed iron founding and agricultural engineering, employed three men, and occupied premises at both Old Alresford and Northington.

Its catchment area took in Swarraton Farm at Northington. One of the housemaids employed in the farmhouse was Katherine Goodall, a labourer's daughter from Wield, so she and William may well have met when he was shoeing at the farm. They were eventually married at Old Alresford in May 1889 and moved in with William's parents at the Post Office. They had one child, Alan, born in 1890.

William worked for Ramptons for about 20 years. Then in 1901 the smithy at Preston Candover fell vacant and he decided to set up on his own account. He had thus only been at Preston for six months before he was called on to adopt his baby nephew.

In 1901 the population of Preston Candover and the neighbouring parish of Nutley amounted to 496 people. (Nutley had become a Chapelry of Preston Candover during the Civil War and from then on the two parishes were effectively treated as one.) Most of the population dwelt in the village at Preston. The other settlements consisted of a hamlet at Axford, and Nutley village which contained only a small church, farmstead and a few cottages.

The scene round the village pond at Preston Candover in the 1900s. The pump was provided for the parish in 1870 under the auspices of Colonel Fitzgerald. The brick steps came to be used as a platform for religious and political meetings and as a place for pedlars to display their wares. A communal grindstone was also provided. Beyond the pond stands the church of St Mary, designed by Arthur Blomfield and consecrated in 1885. One half of the cottage on the left became the home of Walter Murphy and his family in the mid-1930s. (7)

The map opposite shows what the village of Preston Candover looked like in 1910. It was a long straggling settlement. Some of the cottages were built of brick, some timber-framed, others of brick and flint with thatched, tiled or slate roofs, all standing amidst a patchwork of gardens, paddocks and orchards. These paddocks were owned by a variety of people, including the Churchwardens and School Governors, but most of them were rented out to John Thorp the butcher and George Allen the grocer and baker, to form modest farm holdings.

The village contained three fine mansions – Preston House, North and South Hall. The vicarage and the old rectory were also substantial houses.

Spiritual needs were catered for by a small Primitive Methodist Chapel, dating from 1865, and by the parish churches at Nutley and Preston, both dedicated to St Mary. Preston's church had been built in 1885 to replace an existing 17th century building, of which only the chancel now remained and which was used as a mortuary chapel.

The parish possessed two public houses, *The Purefoy Arms* at Preston and *The Crown* at Axford. The village shops comprised a butcher, two grocers – one of whom was also a baker – and a Post Office and general store. The tradesmen included a coal merchant, blacksmith, wheelwright and carpenter, and carrier. To the west of the village on the summit of Tull's Hill stood a small brickworks which was leased to a Basingstoke building company, Mussellwhite and Sapp. Two brothers, Stephen and William Kimber, worked Flockmoor Farm at Axford, though their prime occupation was that of woodmen.

Walter enjoyed a happy boisterous childhood at Preston Candover. He attended the village school which catered for the children of Preston, Nutley and Bradley and had about 130 pupils on the books. Actual attendance was frequently much lower than this, particularly amongst the boys who, depending on the season, would be absent leading horses in the fields, haymaking, stone picking or beating for shooting parties. The pupils, divided into three classes, were

Above left – Walter in about 1903. (8)
Above right – St Mary's Church where he served as a choirboy. (9) Below – The village school which he attended from 1905-10. (10)

The Village

Preston Candover in 1910. The heart of the original Saxon settlement was possibly situated near the old church, rectory and manor farm. By the early 19th century both the church and rectory were in a poor state. The clergy usually lived at South Hall and let the rectory to a labouring family. The Reverend Sumner Wilson, on coming to Preston in 1862, transformed the rectory into a handsome house. He then had a new vicarage built further up the village. This was completed in 1873, whereupon the old rectory was sold off and in 1910 was the home of Doctor Gauge. The old St Mary's was replaced by the new church in 1885.

1. Methodist Chapel
2. Grocer
3. Butcher
4. Carrier
5. Post Office & General Store
6. Grocer and Baker
7. Blacksmith
8. Cycle Agents
9. The Croft
10. Carpenter & Wheelwright
11. The Purefoy Arms
12. Mortuary Chapel (Old St Mary's)
13. Physician, Surgeon, Medical Officer & Public Vaccinator (Old Rectory)
14. Bricklayer

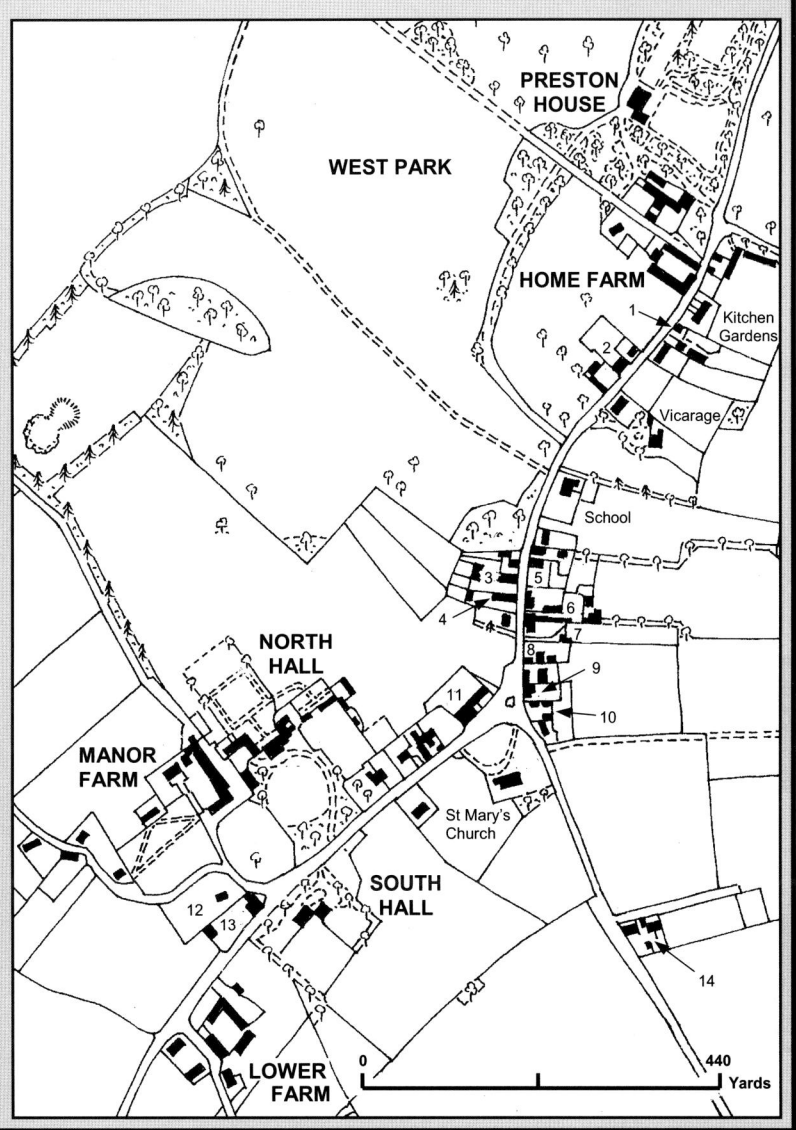

taught by the Headmistress and her three assistants. The Headmistress from 1906-10 was Miss Florence Shayler. She was then in her late twenties. Brought up in Reading, she had first taught at an elementary school in Eastbourne before coming to Preston. Her duties often entailed receiving visits from the wives and daughters of the local gentry. She also had to cope with the daunting presence of the Vicar, the Reverend Sumner Wilson, who would conduct the assembly every morning.

Walter joined in the various social activities such as the Easter Monday athletics meeting, the Boy Scouts' camp, the church choir outing to Bournemouth, and the Christmas Mummers. The most popular event of the year was Club Day which included a fun fair and a march-past from the Medstead Brass Band. Occasionally some special event would occur, as happened on 13 June 1907 when the foundation stone was laid at Moundsmere Manor. This was originally going to be a family affair but when the owner Wilfred Buckley was told the villagers would like to come along and watch, he happily agreed and had a tea laid on for the occasion.

In 1909 Walter's grandmother, Ann Padwick, died after 43 years service as the postmistress at Old Alresford. Her funeral was well-attended, with the postmen of the Alresford district acting as bearers. Amongst the family mourners was Walter's mother. In the years since being widowed, Catherine had become cook for Major Maurice and Lady Portal who lived near Hexham in Northumberland. This may have been the first time Catherine had seen her children since their adoption. Whatever the case, the occasion clearly set her thinking and she subsequently wrote to her siblings to say she now wanted the children back.

This announcement came as a shock to all concerned, for they had always assumed the adoption would be a permanent arrangement. However, Catherine would not be dissuaded and, since neither adop-

Members of the Foresters Friendly Society, gathered in the field behind The Purefoy Arms *on Club Day in 1910. The Reverend Sumner Wilson sits in the centre of the second row, with (left) Eyre Evans Lloyd, the owner of North Hall, and (right) Doctor Osmund Gauge, the resident physician. Seated in the front row, 6th from left, is Jim Colby whose father was tenant at Manor Farm, while seated at far right is Walter Murphy. **(11)***

tion had been put on a legal footing, they had no option but to comply with her wishes. Walter, now in his ninth year, was taken up to King's Cross Station where the Padwicks placed him in the care of the guard. Then, seated alone in the guard's van, he travelled up to York where he was met by his mother who took him on to Hexham. There he was reunited with his sister Kathleen.

In 1913 Catherine remarried, this time to a widower some 10 years her senior named Thomas Winder. He had been a farm worker in Scotland and Northumberland for much of his life, but more latterly had served as Major Portal's gardener. Walter got on well with his stepfather, but he never took to his mother and remained bitterly resentful of her uprooting him from his Hampshire home.

Matters came to a head early in 1915 when he learnt that she intended putting him to work in the local coal mine. He promptly ran away and headed down to Newcastle where he signed on as a cabin boy aboard a coastal trader named the S.S. *Algerba*. It soon became clear he had no future as a sailor for he spent the whole voyage laid up with chronic seasickness and so, when the ship docked at London in May 1915, he was formally discharged. A policeman lent him the train fare to Basingstoke and from there he made his way back to Preston Candover.

In the aftermath of his return to the village, Catherine came to accept that Walter would be a sore trial to her if she forced him to go back to Hexham. What then was to be done with him? Could he perhaps

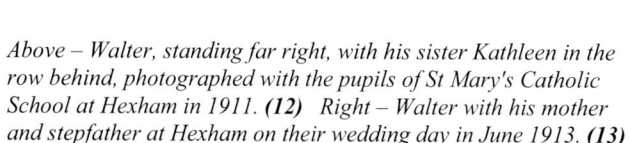

*Above – Walter, standing far right, with his sister Kathleen in the row behind, photographed with the pupils of St Mary's Catholic School at Hexham in 1911. **(12)** Right – Walter with his mother and stepfather at Hexham on their wedding day in June 1913. **(13)***

Above – The Forge Cottage at Preston Candover in the early 1900s. The tall house beyond contained the grocer's shop with bakehouse behind, which belonged to the Allen family. (14)   Right – Walter's cousin, Alan Padwick, with his bride, Florence Fosbury, whose family lived at Axford. They were married in 1914 and thereafter lived with Alan's parents at the Forge Cottage. They were to have two daughters. (15)

work for his uncle at the smithy? William's own son Alan had chosen not to follow his father's trade but had instead become a carpenter and was to spend his life working for the Moundsmere Estate at Preston. Walter, on the other hand, had always taken a keen interest in the smithy and, in the year or so before he left the village, he had been slipping in there when things were quiet and trying his hand at fashioning the odd horseshoe or some other piece of ironwork. It was decided, therefore, that he should be formally apprenticed to his uncle. He was to go on working at the smithy for the next 70 years.

*

The Forge Cottage lay in the heart of the village fronting almost directly onto the street. It was of brick construction, part-thatched and part-tiled. Most of it dated from the 17th century, with a later extension at the front. Behind the cottage lay a long narrow plot of land about an acre in size. The smithy stood on the southern boundary of this plot, some 30 yards back from the street.

The Whitear family had held the smithy as a copyhold tenancy under the Jervoise family of Herriard Park. When the Jervoises decided to sell off their properties in Preston in 1905, the smithy was acquired by the Hope family of Preston House who let it to William Padwick on a yearly tenancy of £12.10.0d. In 1909, however, the Hopes also decided to put some of their land up for sale and so William was able to buy the freehold for £300.

A smithy had stood behind the Forge Cottage since at least 1820, though the building which occupied the site in the 1900s seems to have been built in the late 19th century. It had an L-shaped layout and was constructed of brick and tile with an earth floor, the latter usually covered in broken chalk. There were two forges, one sited in each part of the 'L', plus a hand drill, a long handled iron cutter, a tyre bender, and a floor mandrel for making hoops and rings. The walls were studded with nails, each one allocated to a particular horse, on which the shoes would be hung, ready for when needed.

A wheel-binding plate was located in the yard at the front of the smithy, while harrows, tyres and other items awaiting repair were stacked round the edge. In the meadow behind the smithy stood a large grindstone. Here too William would store coal, clinkers, soot and scrap iron, and park the larger farm implements and wagons. For his transport needs William kept a bicycle and a pony and trap, but most work-related journeys were made on foot.

The smithy was operated by two men – William and an assistant named Harry Holding, who worked at the smithy till the outbreak of war in 1914. Sometimes they would be assisted by an itinerant smith named Billy who usually turned up in the late spring and helped out during the summer months, sleeping in the wood shed and spending his wages every evening at *The Purefoy*. Other assistance would be called upon as needed. Wheelbinding, for instance, was carried out in conjunction with the wheelwright,

The Landowners

During the 19th century the Candover Valley came to be carved up into large estates. Much of the country to the north of Nutley belonged to the Earl of Portsmouth, that to the east of Preston to the Jeffreys and Jervoises. To the west and south a large swath of the valley had come into the possession of the famous banking family, the Barings. Alexander Baring, created Lord Ashburton in 1835, purchased the Grange at Northington in about 1816. He then bought up large tracts of land at Abbotstone and Itchen Stoke in 1818, Brown and Chilton Candover in 1824, and Itchen Abbas in 1835.

Within Preston Candover and Nutley the land came to be largely subdivided between three estates which belonged to the owners of Herriard Park and Preston House, and to the Wardens and Scholars of Winchester College. The latter's holding comprised the Moundsmere Estate. During the medieval period this land had been owned by a religious body, the Priory of Southwark, but following the dissolution of the monasteries the estate had eventually come into the possession of Winchester College who let it to tenants.

Preston House had been built around the end of the 17th century and during the 19th century it was occupied by a succession of landed gentlemen and wealthy merchants. Herriard Park had been acquired early in the 17th century by the Jervoise family. George Purefoy Jervoise, born in 1770, succeeded to the Herriard estate in 1805. He was married to Elizabeth Hall whose family owned the Manor Farms at Preston and Nutley as well as North and South Hall. This land passed to Elizabeth in 1812 and thus came to be included in the Jervoise estates.

On the death of George Purefoy Jervoise in 1847, the estate was split up between different branches of the family. The lands of Preston and Nutley passed to a niece who was married to Thomas Fitzgerald, the owner of Shalstone House in Buckinghamshire. His family moved into North Hall in the 1860s.

During the 1900s the three main estates came up for sale – the Jervoise lands in 1905, the Moundsmere Estate in 1906, and the Preston House Estate in 1909. The ownership of these estates in 1909 is shown on the map. The letters refer to those areas of woodland which were held in hand while the numbers refer to the individual farms.

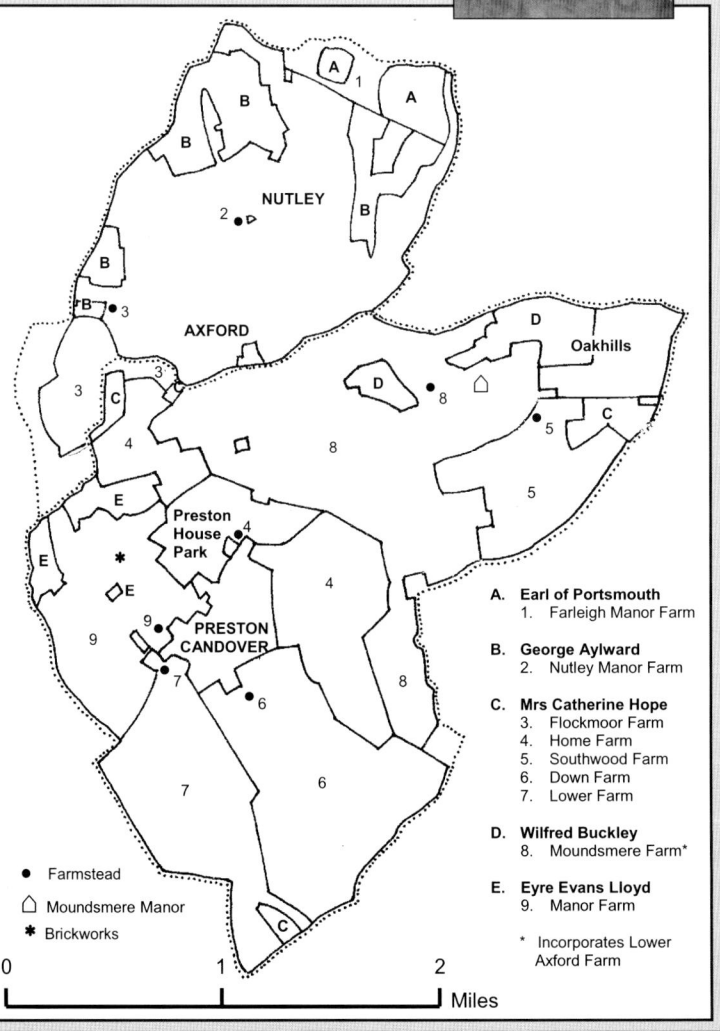

Above – Colonel Fitzgerald with his family at North Hall in about 1886. (16)
Right – George Purefoy Jervoise of Herriard Park. (17)

- Farmstead
- △ Moundsmere Manor
- ✸ Brickworks

A. **Earl of Portsmouth**
   1. Farleigh Manor Farm

B. **George Aylward**
   2. Nutley Manor Farm

C. **Mrs Catherine Hope**
   3. Flockmoor Farm
   4. Home Farm
   5. Southwood Farm
   6. Down Farm
   7. Lower Farm

D. **Wilfred Buckley**
   8. Moundsmere Farm*

E. **Eyre Evans Lloyd**
   9. Manor Farm

* Incorporates Lower Axford Farm

The Whitears

Throughout the 19th century the Preston Candover smithy was run by the Whitear family. Their connection with the village began in 1772 when a Preston girl, Sarah Hall, was married in Tidcombe, Wiltshire to a local man named William Whitear. The couple came to live in Preston where their first son was born in 1774. They were to have eight children, of whom three died in infancy.

William and Ann Whitear in about 1890. (18)

The second son John, born in 1776, took over the smithy. He married a Preston girl Rachel Hedgecock in 1816, with whom he had five children. Like most village tradespeople, the Whitears dabbled in various enterprises. Rachel used the extension at the front of the cottage as a beer shop. John was not only a blacksmith but a farmer too. He worked the meadow behind the smithy as well as a 10 acre allotment out on the road to Wield. He also owned a cottage at Axford which he let to three labourers' families.

Of John and Rachel's five children, three were girls and one of the boys died in infancy. The remaining son Eli commenced working for his father at the smithy. Then in 1851 William Budge, an American Mormon missionary, arrived in the village looking for converts. He enjoyed considerable success amongst the families in the tradesmen and labouring class. Eli Whitear and his sister Elizabeth were two of those converted to the faith and they eventually emigrated to the United States. Eli became a Bishop in the Church of the Latter Day Saints in Morgan, Utah where he died in 1908. John was thus left with no son to whom he could hand on the smithy and so, after his death in 1856, it was taken over by his nephew William.

William was the illegitimate son of John's sister Jemima. He was born in Winchester in 1825 and later came to live at the Forge Cottage in Preston where he was apprenticed at the smithy. He then went to work for James Pitter, the blacksmith and iron founder at Brown Candover. There he met and married Ann Patience, a labourer's daughter. They were to have four children – Thomas, Mary, Eli and William John.

All three boys went to work at the Preston smithy in their teens. Thomas eventually emigrated to Australia where he reputedly acquired a gold mine. Eli and William John left Preston during the 1890s. Ann died in 1897. Thus William ended his days in Preston as a widower with no sons to whom he could hand on the smithy, and so when he died in January 1901, the business was put up for sale.

The village carpenter and wheelwright, Frank Westbrook (left) with his son Fred in about 1920. (19)

Frank Westbrook, and could require the help of up to four men whose rate of pay would be 10d an hour.

The working day was some 12 hours long, six days a week. The day's routine was geared to that of the farm workhorse. The local farmers worked a "one-yoke shift", which meant taking the horse teams out at 7.00am and bringing them back at 3.00pm, with a nosebag feed at noon. William and Harry would thus get up at about 5.00am and go to the stables to put on a set or two before the horses were taken out. Alternatively they could go out to the field during the noon feed or return to the farm in the late afternoon. In between these times they would shoe the horses belonging to the gentry or tradesmen, or see to some item awaiting repair.

William relied on outside suppliers for just a few bulk items. The coal was delivered in a seven ton railway wagon to Medstead Station, from whence it was carted to Preston by the village carrier. The iron was delivered in standard lengths by T.M. Kingdon & Co., a firm of Basingstoke ironmongers. Occasionally William would go into town to purchase factory-made nails, tools, pipes or tanks, as well as

The Hope Family

The Hopes came to the Candover Valley in 1887. Head of the family was Henry John Hope. He had been born in 1839 in York where his father owned a substantial drapery and tailoring business. After his father's death in 1859, Henry appears to have taken charge of the business for a few years, but it was then sold off and he became a leisured gentleman, living off the income from his investments. In 1876 he married Catherine Fanny Burr, the daughter of a wealthy Yorkshire attorney and solicitor, and the principal beneficiary of a family trust.

For a few years Henry and Catherine lived in the north of England and enjoyed a cultivated lifestyle. They had three sons – William, Oliver and John. By 1887 they wanted a more permanent home and, by drawing on the Burr family trust, they were able to purchase the Preston House Estate. Henry soon became a dominating presence in the locality, throwing himself with enthusiasm into the role of country squire and J.P. A prime example of this occurred each Sunday morning when, having taken his place at the front of the church, he would turn round, put his monocle in his eye, and scan the pews to check whether any of his employees was absent.

At first the estate comprised nearly 1400 acres and included the Home, Southwood, Bradley Lower and Wield Farms. Henry had purchased the Preston House Estate during the worst years of the agricultural depression, but the Burr family trust cushioned the family from its effects and even allowed them to acquire additional land. One acquisition was the Down Farm, which they bought in the sale of the Jervoise lands in Preston in 1905. They also acquired Preston Lower Farm from the Lainson family.

After Henry died in 1905, the family's debts caught up with them and in 1909 Catherine put Preston House up for sale, together with about 1660 acres of the estate. The sale was not wholly successful. Catherine thus let the house and in 1910 mortgaged the land that remained to her. In 1913 work commenced on a new house for her, situated at the southern end of the village and to be known as Preston Grange. Work was interrupted by the outbreak of war and it was not until 1920 that she was finally able to move in. She died there in 1936.

The Hopes' sons all attended Winchester College. William displeased his father while at Oxford and emigrated to Canada. Oliver qualified as a solicitor. He was twice married and, with his second wife, came to live at Wieldwood House in Wield where during the 1930s he farmed some 300 acres. He died in 1949.

The East Front of Preston House in about 1900. **(20)**

John went to Sandhurst, from where he was gazetted to The King's Royal Rifle Corps. He saw service in Ireland, India and Cyprus, and during the First World War he was awarded the CBE and DSO. He later attained the rank of Brigadier-General and served as ADC to the King. He retired from military service in 1938, though during the war he served as Commander of the 3rd Battalion Hampshire Home Guard.

He remained a bachelor and during the 1920s he came to live at Preston Grange. He always took a close interest in the village. As a young man he formed a troop of Boy Scouts. In later years he served on the Basingstoke RDC and was at one time Chairman of the Housing Committee. He was President of the Cricket Club and Village Hall Committee, and Vice President of the local branch of the British Legion. A keen antiquarian, he devoted much time to studying the history of Preston Candover. He was also an enthusiastic huntsman and wrote *A History of Hunting in Hampshire*, published in 1950. He died in 1970.

Brigadier-General John Frederic Roundell Hope, CBE, DSO, in 1951. **(21)**

The Preston Candover smithy in about 1910, with William Padwick (left) and his assistant Harry Holding. (22)

items like cement, oil or carbide. But on the whole the bulk of items were still fashioned at the smithy, right down to the smallest pin, bolt or rivet.

William and Harry employed a wide range of skills in their work. A key technique was welding which involved heating metals to a temperature where they would fuse together on contact. They did this by heating the metal parts in the forge and then hammering them together on the anvil, and repeating the process until no join was visible. This technique was used in wheelbinding, in making chains and traces, and in reinforcing tools where the metal had worn thin. This process was known as "lining" and was regularly employed on pickaxes and fold bars (an iron rod used by the shepherd to pierce holes in the ground for inserting hurdle stakes). A related technique was soldering which William employed for the repair of more delicate domestic items such as oil lamps, kettles and kitchen utensils.

The accounts of the Preston Candover smithy provide a detailed picture of how it operated in the years between 1910 and 1914. During those five years the business earned a total of £1223, an annual average of £245 (Graph 1).

The map here shows the towns and country parishes within about eight miles of Preston Candover and identifies those places which, according to the trade directory of 1907, had a smithy. Of the six parishes adjacent to Preston and Nutley, three of them had a smithy – these being Bradley, Brown Candover and Dummer. At that date Basingstoke had four smithies, New Alresford three. Within the district as a whole, there were 23 smithies.

Each smithy thus operated within a very restricted catchment area. In the case of the Preston smithy, the business derived over 90% of its income between

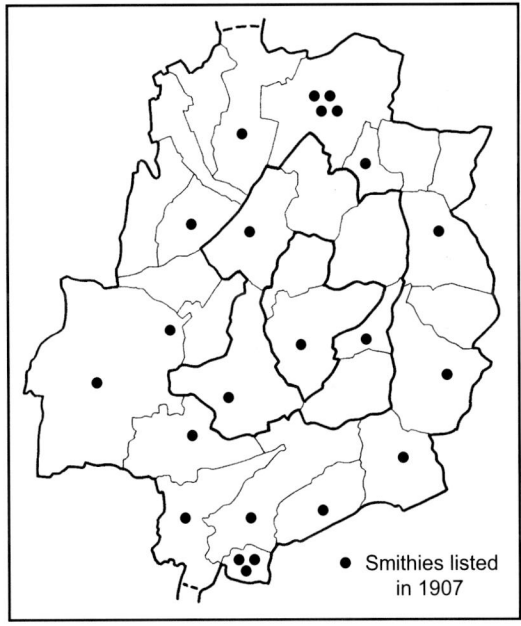

1910-14 from customers who lived in (or were responsible for properties within) the parishes of Preston Candover and Nutley. Even where customers were based outside the area, the work they brought to the Preston blacksmith was usually required for some job they were undertaking in the locality. These customers included the Highway Board, the Basingstoke building contractors, Mussellwhite and Sapp, and a contractor named Mullens and Sons, based in Bath, who were engaged in digging a well at Preston during the first half of 1914.

From 1910-14 the Preston blacksmith undertook work for a total of 77 customers. They were drawn from a wide spectrum of rural life – gentry, clergy, farmers, shopkeepers, builders, carriers, wood dealers, the School Governors, Parish Council and Churchwardens, the Foresters Friendly Society and

Horses & Engines

The blacksmith was just one of a host of tradesmen who had a vested interest in the preservation of "horse power". For during the 19th century the horse had come to play a crucial role in both farming and transport.

For centuries oxen had provided the motive power in farming but by 1900 the horse had largely taken over this role. At first these animals were of indifferent quality but in the 1860s there was a move towards the breeding of better animals. Breed societies were established and these led to the development of such heavy horses as the Shire, Clydesdale and Suffolk.

Furthermore, although the railways had put the long distance coaches out of business, the conveyance of goods and passengers to and from the railway station still relied on horse-drawn vehicles. By 1900 the volume of such traffic was greater than ever before and it encompassed a multiplicity of vehicles – the butcher's cart, bread cart, brewer's dray, miller's van, governess' cart, dog cart (for shooting parties), private omnibus, barouche, landau and various types of gig.

The most widespread form of mechanical road transport was the pedal cycle. It had become enormously popular following the invention of the safety cycle in the 1880s and by 1900 its users were supported by a network of cycle shops. The development of steam-powered road transport, however, had been hampered by highly restrictive legislation. This in turn had held back the early development in Britain of the internal combustion engine. In 1896 the motoring enthusiasts' lobby finally succeeded in bringing about a major relaxation in these restrictions and this at last made steam road haulage a commercial proposition. One of the first firms in the country to take advantage of this fact was the Hampshire engineering firm of Tasker and Sons of Andover. By 1902 they had produced the first of their "Little Giant" series, for which they also produced purpose-built trailers. Other manufacturers, most notably the Foden company, developed the steam wagon.

The development of steam road haulage took place in parallel with that of oil-powered vehicles. The most prominent form of such transport was the private car which during the 1900s was seen as little more than a rich man's plaything. It could be extremely temperamental, both to start and drive. Its tyres wore out quickly and the fuel varied greatly in quality. And, since there was no network of repair, servicing and fuel supply, the smallest trip could be beset with hazards. While these circumstances prevailed, the car posed little threat to horse-drawn transport.

The advent of the light steam-powered tractor offered a practical alternative to the horse in drawing farm implements. Yet more possibilities beckoned with the advent of the internal combustion engine and throughout the 1900s a large number of engineering companies tried their hand at developing a practical oil-powered tractor. A wide range of models was produced but British farmers generally showed little interest and so the horse remained the prime source of motive power in the countryside.

---

the Preston Candover Cricket Club. The gentry included the major landowners who managed their farms directly like the Hopes at Preston House and Wilfred Buckley at Moundsmere Manor. They also included such wealthy gentlemen as the Reverend Sumner Wilson, Eyre Evans Lloyd and Charles Alexander Hall who resided at North and South Hall respectively, and the resident physician, Doctor Osmund Gauge who lived at the old rectory. Amongst the tradesmen there were men such as the butcher John Thorp and the grocer George Allen who also farmed land in the parish. However, despite the variety of social groups served by the Preston blacksmith, his income was very dependent on a few key customers. Overall, the top 20% of customers provided 81% of income.

William also performed a host of minor jobs for families of the labouring class such as fashioning steel tips for a pair of boots, sharpening an axe, or perhaps soldering a saucepan. These jobs were done in a spirit of good neighbourliness and were paid for

INCOME EARNED FROM DIFFERENT TYPES OF CUSTOMER, 1910-14

Major Landowners	36%
Tenant Farmers	30%
Clergy & Other Gentry	17%
Tradesmen	15%
Institutions	2%

The "Major Landowners" are those members of the gentry who managed their farms directly. The "Other Gentry" are those whose estates did not include farmland or who let their farms to tenants. The "Institutions" include the Post Office, Highway Board, Parish Council, Churchwardens, School Governors, the Foresters Friendly Society and the Cricket Club.

INCOME EARNED FROM DIFFERENT TYPES OF WORK, 1910-14

Horseshoeing	63%
Farm Work	13%
Construction Work	11%
Wheelbinding	5%
Tools	4%
Other	4%

Left – A horse-drawn cart loaded with faggots standing outside The Purefoy Arms. *(23)*

Below – Harry Prouten on his tricycle outside The Purefoy Arms *with Jesse Roper, the landlord. Harry came to Preston in about 1900 and worked at the brickyard. After the yard closed down, he became a roadman and gravedigger, and used the tricycle for riding to work. (24)*

through an informal bartering system, perhaps for vegetables, fruit, eggs, honey or timber, or perhaps in the form of a "good turn".

The type of work undertaken by the Preston blacksmith can be grouped into five main categories: shoeing; farm work (which covers work involving farm implements, carts and machinery); construction work; wheelbinding; and tools. An "Other" category is added to cover the host of miscellaneous tasks which the blacksmith also undertook.

*

Preston Candover in the early 1900s was still home to what was basically a horse-drawn society, though change was clearly in the air. The parish lay within the ambit of Basingstoke, being part of the Basingstoke Poor Law Union and the Basingstoke Rural District. Basingstoke was the market town for the area and by 1900 its influence on country life was steadily expanding. The Basingstoke Post Office organised the local mail and telegraph service and by 1910 it had also laid on a public telephone, installed in a greenhouse next to the Post Office. The service once provided by Preston's village tailor and shoemaker was now met by the sales reps from the Basingstoke department stores who would regularly visit the parish, bearing their samples of off-the-peg clothes and shoes in a wagonette.

During these years Preston acquired its own cycle shop, run by two brothers, William and Albert Hall. They came from Bentworth where their father had worked as a carpenter. They moved to Preston in the 1890s and lived with their widowed mother in a cottage next door to the smithy. The boys initially went into domestic service, but in about 1907 they set up the cycle shop in a shed at the front of the property. From there they sold not only bicycles but spares, brake blocks, puncture outfits and other accessories.

Clem Westbrook, a wood dealer and a minor customer of the Preston Candover blacksmith, with his wife Lucy and their children outside their home, Church Farm Cottage, at Wield. Clem was a notable brewer of homemade wine and his cottage was often packed out with friends from the surrounding parishes, including Walter Murphy, who would gather there to enjoy a chat and a sing-song over a jug of wine. (25)

The Buckleys

Wilfred Buckley was born in 1873 in Edgbaston, Birmingham. After attending Giggleswick School in Yorkshire, he worked in the family business, handling the transhipment of Birmingham manufactures. He was then sent to America to manage the firm's New York office. There he met a Fifth Avenue heiress named Bertha Terrell. They were married in 1898 and had one daughter Janet, born in 1901.

Wilfred returned to England with his family and in 1906 he bought the Moundsmere Estate at Preston Candover. There he built a Palladian style mansion which he named Moundsmere Manor. He took a keen interest in the management of his estate, and introduced several innovations, including a dairy which produced milk of exceptional hygienic quality.

Moundsmere Manor, designed by Reginald Blomfield and built between 1907-9. (26)

The dairy came about because, shortly after the Buckleys' arrival in England, Janet contracted tubercular glands. Although she recovered successfully, it was imperative that in future she should only have milk guaranteed free of bovine tubercle. In the United States such "certified" milk was widely available but in England it was unknown. Wilfred decided, therefore, to set up his own dairy. He did this to such effect that the venture soon developed into a commercial undertaking, the milk being bottled and taken by train each day to London, where it was distributed amongst the West End stores.

Such initiatives as the Moundsmere dairy were of considerable interest to medical practitioners and others who were at that time campaigning to improve the hygienic quality of the milk supply. Wilfred himself was soon drawn into playing an active role in the movement. He penned letters to the press, gave lectures, and lobbied Government over milk legislation. In 1915 he founded the National Clean Milk Society (NCMS).

During the First World War Wilfred played an active role in securing the nation's food supply, and in 1917 he was appointed Director of Milk Supplies at the Ministry of Food. His chief responsibility was to set fair prices, but he also used his position to promote the clean milk cause. In 1920 he was awarded the CBE.

During the 1920s Wilfred, as Chairman of the NCMS, continued to promote the cause by means of lectures, conferences and demonstrations at agricultural shows. His efforts were generally derided by the dairy industry. This never deflected him from the cause but he did become depressed at the widespread apathy which developed during the late 1920s. He finally wound up the NCMS in 1928, though he continued to play an active role in the movement.

The Buckleys supported many social and sporting events in Preston Candover. In the early 1920s Bertha served as County Councillor for the Dummer Division. She took a close interest in the village school and, during her time as a school manager, she introduced a school meals service and a Milk Club.

Wilfred always displayed a keen interest in literature and art, but his real passion was collecting antique glass. Over the years he built up a sizeable collection which attracted considerable interest amongst fellow collectors. During the late 1920s he wrote a series of specialist books on the subject. He also took part in organising several major exhibitions. All this brought a number of distinguished visitors to Moundsmere, of whom the most eminent was Queen Mary who made a private visit in 1931.

Wilfred died at a London Nursing Home in October 1933, following an operation for cancer. For a time Bertha managed the estate on her own and carried forward some unfinished projects on the glass collection. In 1935 she sold the estate to Herman Andreae and went to live at Ham Common in Surrey where she died in 1937.

Wilfred Buckley in about 1920. (27)

Above – The Vicar's daughter, Emily Wilson, pondering on whether to purchase a horse from Bob Jones, a horse dealer from Wield, near the old rectory at Preston Candover. (28)   Right – A noonday nosebag feed. (29)

Steam-powered tractors were also much in evidence. They were used extensively in 1907-8 for hauling building materials up to Moundsmere for the new mansion. One was employed by Musselwhite and Sapp to cart the bricks from the yard on Tull's Hill. Unfortunately it was this innovation which brought about the end of brickmaking in the village. For the driver used to stop at the bottom of Brick Kiln Lane close by North Hall and stoke up the boiler till he had a sufficient head of steam to climb up the hill to the yard. The resulting smoke and sparks greatly annoyed Eyre Lloyd, the owner of both North Hall and the brickyard, and he finally put a stop to the problem by closing down the brickyard.

As for motor vehicles, by 1910 there were at least four car owners in Preston Candover. They included Wilfred Buckley, Doctor Gauge, Eyre Lloyd and Charles Hall. None of these developments in mechanical road transport, however, posed much threat to the farriery side of the Preston Candover smithy.

During the years 1910-14 the Preston blacksmith shod on average 110 individual horses each year and of these, 64% were farm workhorses. Moundsmere Farm had about 17 horses, Home Farm 11, the Down Farm and Preston Manor Farm 10. In addition to these, there were cobs and ponies kept for the personal use of the farmer and his family. About 20 horses were kept by the tradesmen, some for drawing delivery vans and carts, others for farm work.

PRICES CHARGED FOR SHOEING 1910-14	
Hunters & Carriage Horses	4/- per set
Farm Workhorses	3/- .. ..
Tradesmen's Horses	3/- .. ..
Ponies	2/6d ..
Donkeys	2/- .. ..

HORSE-RELATED SERVICES

In 1912 William Padwick earned £142.7s.9d from making and fitting new horseshoes. The income earned from other horse-related services came to £6.13s.1d. This sum was made up of the following services:

Removes (70%) – removing the shoe, trimming the feet, and nailing the shoe back on.
Charge: 6d per shoe

Steeling (10%) – forging a layer of steel into the shoe to give it extra strength and stop it wearing out too fast. Often necessary where the horse was employed on the roads.
Charge: 1½d per shoe

Trimming (8%) – pulling off the shoes and trimming the feet without fitting a new shoe immediately. Mainly done with hunters at the end of the season.
Charge: 2d a foot

Leathers (5%) – placing a leather pad across the foot and nailing the shoe into place. Often done where the horse had a bruised sole.
Charge: 6d a foot

Rough-Nailing (3%) – removing two of the nails from a shoe and fitting special frost nails to prevent the horse from slipping in icy weather.
Charge: 1d a foot

Nailing (2%) – tightening the shoes without removing them.
Charge: 2d a shoe

Screwing (2%) – drilling holes in the shoe so that studs could be inserted as required, to prevent the horse slipping in icy weather.
Charge: 3d a shoe

In 1912 William was also called on by John Thorp, the butcher, to deal with a case of "seedy toe", a disease which caused the inner hoof wall to degenerate. William cleaned out the cavity, dressed it with Stockholm tar, and packed it with "toe", a material made from hemp.

The Farming Scene

Times were extremely harsh for country people during the early part of the 19th century but by 1850 matters had started to improve and for some 20 years thereafter British farmers enjoyed a period of considerable prosperity.

At that time the farming economy of the Hampshire downs was based primarily on sheep. The arable fields were sown with a four course rotation of swedes or turnips, barley or oats, grass and wheat, and with a catch crop of vetches or clover inserted between the wheat and turnips. During the winter months the sheep were kept in hurdle folds on the fields of turnips, vetches or clover. Lambing took place in February, the shepherd living out amongst the flocks in a hut on wheels. June was the shearing month. In early October the lambs were taken to market while the ewes were moved back onto the arable land in readiness for meeting the ram in November. The system, known as the "Golden Hoof", produced two annual harvests, one of wool and one of meat. At the same time the sheep, in manuring the arable fields, secured a good crop of wheat as part of the rotation.

The decline of this system began in the 1870s with the importation of cheap wheat and barley from America. At the same time huge quantities of frozen meat, butter, cheese and wool came to be imported from Australia, New Zealand, and South America. In country districts this led to constantly falling prices, bankruptcies, rents going unpaid, and land, buildings and equipment left to decay. Marginal farming areas, such as the high chalk downland of Hampshire, were simply abandoned.

In time the reduction in both the farm acreage and the number of farmers, helped the survivors to adjust to a lower volume of production. After 1890 there was a general rise in world food prices which assisted British farmers. Thus by the 1900s it was possible to make a decent living, provided the farmer managed his holding efficiently.

For centuries the prime farm implements had been the plough, harrow and roller. All other farm work had been performed with hand tools. Both implements and tools were made locally, with the ironwork supplied by the blacksmith. During the 18th century the industrial revolution began to open up opportunities for new techniques and equipment, and by 1900 the farmer had a wide range of implements available to assist him in his work – iron ploughs, harrows, ring rollers, seed drills, horsehoes, sheaf-binding reapers, grassmowers, tedders, swath turners, side-delivery rakes, haysweeps – all of which required servicing by the local blacksmith.

The farmer could also make use of a wide range of barn machinery, such as chaff cutters, oil cake crushers, and mills for chopping up turnips or mangels. Pride of place went to the threshing machine, driven by a portable steam engine and used in conjunction with a horse or steam powered elevator for transferring the threshed straw to the rick. Only the larger farms owned such machinery; most farmers employed contractors. By 1900, however, this situation had begun to change with the advent of small stationary engines powered by acetylene gas and later by oil.

Between 15 and 25 horses would be shod each year for the gentry. About five of these appear to have been hunters. However, it is not clear just how consistent William was in identifying the different types of horses in the accounts, so the number may have been somewhat higher. The other types of horse included hacks and carriage horses as well as animals like Morby who was employed in drawing the lawnmower and carrying out other light work about the gardens of Preston House. The Reverend Sumner Wilson had a disabled son named Arthur and so, in addition to a carriage horse, he also kept two donkeys for drawing Arthur's wheelchair round the parish.

In 1910-14 William and Harry made and fitted an average of 3713 horseshoes per year, of which about 65% were for farm workhorses and 15% for tradesmen's horses. Shoeing dominated the day's work. As soon as one set had been put on, the smith proceeded to make a new set, ready for when they were needed. The frequency with which the horses were shod varied a good deal, but amongst the farms of Preston and Nutley the horses employed on the land appear to have been shod every six or seven weeks. The horses used on the roads required shoeing far more frequently – perhaps every fortnight to three weeks. One such horse was listed in the accounts as "Milk Horse". It belonged to Moundsmere Farm and was employed each day in taking the milk to the railway station at Herriard. Milk Horse was shod 16 times during 1912 and the average interval between sessions was about 21 days.

For the Preston blacksmith, therefore, his core work lay in shoeing the farm workhorses. This work was carried out on an informal rota, with the horses shod over a period of a week to 10 days, and with two or three horses shod each day. This effectively spread out the work between the farms and allowed the smith to fit in the needs of the gentry and tradesmen.

*

A flock of sheep being led along Berrydown Lane in 1913 by Alfred Thomas Earwicker. Alfred (more commonly known as Fred) was born in Itchen Stoke in 1899. In later life he became a builder and decorator, and set up his own business in Preston in 1947. In the 1950s he also provided a funeral director's service and for a time Walter Murphy acted as one of his pall bearers. Fred died in 1981. (30)

The estates of Preston Candover and Nutley were divided between eight farms of 200-1000 acres in extent. They had mostly acquired their present form following the enclosure of the common fields and downland of Preston and Nutley in 1820. The prosperous years of the mid-19th century saw many improvements in the valley, with new farmsteads built at Lower Axford and Preston Home Farm, the fields enlarged, and all but the steepest slopes of Preston Down ploughed up. Such improvements gradually ceased with the onset of the farming depression. The worst area of dereliction in the locality was Chilton Down, just to the southwest of Preston Candover, where some 200 acres of land was allowed to revert to rough pasture, ragwort and scrub. Other areas were given over to game coverts and parkland. About 130 acres came to be included in the parkland at Preston House while another 90 acres on Preston Down were converted into a golf course.

The improved outlook for British farmers in the early 1900s was exemplified in Preston Candover by Wilfred Buckley. Following his acquisition of the Moundsmere Estate in 1906, he was to become a notable progressive farmer. He pioneered the keeping of proper records and from these he concluded that the traditional breeding flock of sheep was a loss making venture. He thus abandoned the flock and

FARM-RELATED WORK IN 1912

Total income from farm-related work: £20. 7s. 4d
This sum was made up from servicing:

Farm implements	61%
Farm vehicles	22%
Farm equipment	10%
Harnessing	7%

Income from servicing farm implements: £12. 9s. 2d
This sum was made up from servicing implements which were used in:

Ploughing & cultivating	62%
Haymaking	18%
Sowing & planting	16%
Harvesting	3%
Other processes	1%

Above – James Boshier, farm bailiff at Lower Axford Farm. (31)
Left – Grass cutting at Upper Farm, Bradley. (32)

Right – A binder at work at Upper Farm, Bradley. (33) Below – Threshing at Preston Candover in 1897. The man in the bowler hat is probably Adam Wilson, a threshing contractor, who lived at Bradley. (34)

instead bought lambs each summer and sold them the following year after shearing. And, while most farms kept pigs, poultry and dairy cattle just to meet local needs, Buckley developed a farming regime which included a herd of 200 pedigree Berkshire pigs, a flock of 1000 laying hens, and a herd of 100 milking cows from which he produced milk of exceptional hygienic quality. He also employed such innovations as gas engines and a steam-powered tractor.

The servicing of farm vehicles and machinery brought in 13% of the Preston blacksmith's income between 1910-14, most of which was earned from servicing farm implements. The remainder came from servicing carts, wagons, sack carts and wheelbarrows, and from making all the different rings and traces used in harnessing. William also made nose rings for bulls and pigs, and carried out repairs to mangers, troughs, bushels, elevators and cake crackers.

The work involving farm implements mainly comprised the servicing of ploughs, rollers, harrows and haymaking machinery. Such work encompassed not only the implement but its accessories too. William would, for example, repair the small curved spanner which was carried on the plough and used to make adjustments. He also purchased a special file which the farmer carried on the grassmower for sharpening the edges of the triangular blades. The servicing of carts and wagons generally involved the manufacture of small items such as lynch pins, washers, eyes, hooks, pins and staples. William also provided the skids, drugbats and chains used for braking the wagon when a steep incline had to be negotiated.

*

The most important source of income for the Preston blacksmith, after horseshoeing and farm work, was construction-related work. This came about through the routine maintenance of the large houses, cottages, outbuildings and other structures in the parish. Nearly all of it was derived from the gentry, either from orders placed directly or via orders placed by Mussellwhite and Sapp who were regularly engaged by Mrs Hope on repairs to various cottages and barns. Some of these orders related to plumbing, guttering, drains and wells, others to doors and windows. Wherever Mussellwhite and Sapp installed new doors and windows in a cottage, they would call on William to provide the hinges, latches and

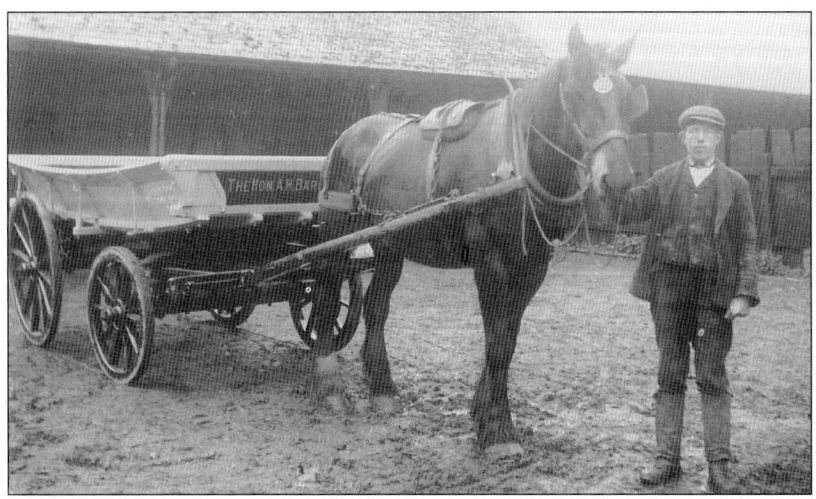

A local farm wagon in about 1910. Holding the reins is John Smith, the carpenter's son at Brown Candover, who later became Walter Murphy's brother-in-law. After serving on the Western Front, John returned to Brown Candover where he worked for the Council, tending the roadside verges up through the valley. He married Ada Adams, a gamekeeper's daughter, in 1924. They had one daughter, Esme. (35)

A newly built house at Nutley (with Alan Padwick standing at the far end of the line of workmen). Much of the ironwork used in its construction would have been provided by the Preston Candover blacksmith. (36)

CONSTRUCTION WORK IN 1912	
Total income from construction work: £28.16s. 6d	
This sum was made up from servicing the following types of property:	
Gentlemen's residences	38%
Farmhouses & cottages	27%
Farmsteads	28%
Church & school property	7%
and from work involving the following items:	
Stoves, kitcheners, flues, chimneys & boilers	34%
Plumbing, gutters, drains & wells	14%
Doors & windows	14%
Structural features	9%
Gates	11%
Fences	8%
Other	10%

catches. Construction income, however, was principally earned from making repairs to fireplaces, kitchen ranges, stoves, stack pipes and chimneys. William would also replace firebricks, cement hearths, clean flues, and sweep chimneys. This was the prime service required by the Churchwardens and School Governors.

In most years wheelbinding only brought in about 5% of total income. The need for wheelbinding arose because wooden wheels were subjected to considerable wear and tear and over time the iron tyres would work loose on their wooden rims. William was therefore called upon either to make and fit a wholly new tyre, or to remove the existing tyre and cut and reweld it to a slightly smaller circumference, a process known as "cutting and shutting". For both processes the tyre had to be welded (or "shut") by heating the two ends in the forge and then hammering them together on the anvil until they were properly fused. The tyre then had to be heated on a fire specially prepared in the yard, from where it could be carried across to the wooden wheel waiting on the wheelbinding plate and hammered into place.

About half of the income earned from the servicing and repair of hand tools came from the farmers, mainly for sharpening, lining or fitting new handles to prongs, billhooks, scythes, turnip pickers, hoes, fold bars, posthole bars and rakes. Another notable customer for such work was the Highway Board. Whenever their men were working on the public roads in the parish, they would bring a steady stream of tools to the smithy for repair, especially pickaxes.

WHEELBINDING WORK IN 1912	
Total income from wheelbinding: £5.14s. 1d	
This sum was made up from servicing the wheels on:	
Farm carts & wagons	71%
Tradesmen's vehicles	26%
Garden wheelbarrows	3%
and from:	
Making & fitting new tyres	49%
Cutting & shutting existing tyres	42%
Other work	9%

OTHER TYPES OF WORK IN 1912	
Total income from other types of work: £8.17s. 0d	
This sum was made up from work which involved:	
Pumps & stationary engines	30%
Domestic items	23%
Horse-drawn carriages, traps, carts & vans, & garden wheelbarrows	20%
Supply of materials	10%
Implements used in gardening, sports ground maintenance, & road repairs	9%
Motor cars & pedal cycles	7%
Traction engines & tractors powered by steam or oil	1%

The "Other" category mainly comprised the servicing of carriages and tradesmen's vans, and repairing pumps and stationary engines. It also included making repairs to garden implements, especially lawnmowers, and to such domestic items as frying pans, fish kettles, coffee pots, oil lamps, candlesticks, mangles and watering cans. It included soldering a gun barrel for the Hopes, a medical instrument for Doctor Gauge, and a sausage grinder for the Thorps. And there were times when William's customers asked him to obtain materials for them, such as oil, carbide, lice powder, peasticks but especially Stockholm tar which was widely used for tending wounds on farm livestock.

This then was the nature of the blacksmith's business at Preston Candover at a time when it was still geared to the needs of a horse-drawn society. It was this way of life, of course, which was to be overturned in the years to come.

The Wilsons

The Reverend Sumner Wilson's family hailed from Westmorland. His father had come down to Queen's College, Oxford and had then gone on to become a Canon of Winchester Cathedral and Vicar of Holy Rood in Southampton. Sumner was his eldest son. Born in 1832, he graduated at Christchurch, Oxford and was ordained in 1856. A year later he married Agnes Tillwood Theobald, the daughter of a Winchester magistrate and landowner. He then served as Curate of Durley near Bishopstoke, before coming to Preston Candover in 1862.

The Vicarage, built for the Wilsons in 1873. (37)

Preston and Nutley had previously suffered from a long period of neglect but under Sumner's guidance the school was improved, the graveyard extended, the old rectory transformed into a handsome house, and a fine new vicarage built. His prime ambition, however, was to have a new church built at Preston and this he finally achieved in 1885.

Sumner was a regular visitor at the school where he gave lessons in scripture, dictation, reading, spelling and arithmetic. At one time he took on the duty of attendance officer. Every Christmas a party would be held at the school where he would distribute cloaks and smocks as presents and give out books as prizes for good conduct.

He served as Chairman of the Parish Vestry and later the Parish Council. He was a very keen antiquarian and enjoyed studying the history of the parish. He contributed to the Victoria County History for Hampshire and built up a valuable collection of books.

His wife Agnes was also a regular visitor at the school and took singing lessons once a week. She was the church organist for 30 years, trained the choir and taught in the Sunday School. She was also a keen supporter of the Mothers' Union.

Sumner and Agnes had five children – George, Anna, William, Emily and Arthur. George became a clergyman and was Vicar of Woodmancott with Popham from 1898-1915. During his time there he frequently came over to Preston to assist his father in his duties. He subsequently served as Rector of Bramdean and Chaplain of St John's Hospital, Winchester.

Anna married a clergyman, the Reverend Alfred Tanner, in 1885. Emily remained at home till her mid-thirties when in 1902 she married James Anderson and went to live at Bournemouth. The marriage proved to be happy but brief and after James' death, she returned to Preston and had a large house built along the road to Axford which she called Fawkners. In their last years, her parents moved out of the vicarage and came to live with her. Sumner died in 1917, Agnes a year later.

Arthur was a very bright young man and attended Selwyn House, Oxford where he graduated in 1891. At about that time, however, he fell seriously ill, possibly through contracting polio, and was left paralysed in his legs and the right side of his body. Thereafter he lived with his parents and later with Emily, and rode about the village in a donkeychair. He was never heard to complain of his disability, but devoted his time to being a private tutor to local families and a gentle observer of village life. He died in 1935.

Emily lived on at Fawkners and became a leading light in village affairs. She was secretary of the WI and a Foundation Trustee of the village hall. She helped form the Preston Candover and District Nursing Association in 1916 and served as secretary till 1948. It was very much through her influence that the village succeeded in the 1950s in obtaining a resident District Nurse. She also served as secretary to Preston's Infant Welfare Clinic, as Enrolling Member of the Mothers' Union, and as School Manager till she was in her 90s. She died in 1959.

The Reverend Sumner Wilson and his wife Agnes in 1907. (38)

Between the Wars

On his return to the Forge Cottage in May 1915, Walter soon settled back into the social life of Preston Candover. As an apprentice at the smithy, his wages were 5/- a week and outside of working hours, he was able to lead a fairly carefree existence, roistering with the other youths of the parish. Then one afternoon he was sent down to Brown Candover to carry out some task up in the belfry of the parish church. From there he spied a young woman visiting one of the graves in the churchyard. On making enquiries he learnt she was Laurie Smith, the daughter of the village carpenter.

Laurie's mother belonged to the family of George Jones, the carrier at Brown Candover. She had been in domestic service for much of her life and, since she did not want a large family, she deliberately delayed getting married till she was 40. This proved a wise move for, when she did finally get married to John Smith in 1895, she had three children within the first five years. They were John, Hilda and Laurie. Hilda was a bright lively girl while Laurie was a shy quiet goody-goody, as exemplified in the numerous certificates and prize books she acquired for good attendance at Sunday School.

Both girls went into domestic service. Hilda secured good posts at Warwick and Kingston, and on one occasion was able to travel with her employer to the south of France. Laurie's posts were at Lingfield near East Grinstead, Belgrave Square, and Northanger. Her opportunities, however, were constantly thwarted because her mother was frequently ill and Laurie, being the youngest daughter, was expected to resign her post and come home to act as carer. It was on one such occasion that she was espied in the churchyard by Walter Murphy.

Above top – The Purefoy Arms some time between the wars, now with a car parked on its forecourt. *(39)* *Above* – John Smith with his wife Jane and daughter Laurie in about 1920. *(40)* *Right* – Laurie and Hilda Smith in about 1919. *(41)*

Matters progressed from there and they were married at Brown Candover in August 1921. They were to have one daughter, also named Laurie. During the early 1920s they lived in a succession of cottages, rented mostly from farmers in Preston and Chilton Candover. Then in 1926 they secured a cottage near Manor Farm at Preston where they stayed for the next eight years. On completing his apprenticeship, Walter's wages were 50/- a week, which he supplemented with gardening, grave digging, sweeping chimneys, and general odd job work.

Walter always showed a keen interest in gadgetry. When he was eight he was given a magic lantern and enjoyed many an evening sitting out in the washhouse with his friends, projecting the pictures onto the large bare wall. In his late teens he acquired a pedal cycle and for a time took a keen interest in photography. Then in the early 1920s wireless became his passion. He would regularly meet up with other enthusiasts in Basingstoke at the premises of W.E. Carter & Son who, though primarily harness makers, also stocked wireless parts. With these Walter would fashion his own crystal sets. Then, with earphones clamped upon his head, he would sit in the cottage of an evening, demanding silence from his family while he tuned the cat's whisker. Naturally his wife and daughter found this hobby sorely trying but he was sometimes able to sell the sets for about £10, so it was at least an extra source of much needed income.

In 1930 Walter decided to use some of his extra earnings to buy a motorcycle and with this the family were able to indulge in pleasure outings. One particular destination for such visits was a lodge at the entrance to an estate called Swanmore Park near Southampton where Walter's mother now lived. The Portals had moved to Swanmore in 1920. Catherine's second husband, Thomas Winder, died there in 1922. Walter's sister Kathleen had remained with their mother. She was married in the early 1920s but, after

*Above – Walter Murphy and Laurie Smith in about 1920. **(42)***
*Below – Laurie and her baby daughter at Cannon's Down, an isolated shepherd's cottage, situated about a mile to the south of the village. This was the Murphys' first home. **(43)***

*Walter, young Laurie, and their dogs Toby and Queenie, in the graveyard of the old St Mary's Church at Preston Candover in 1930. **(44)***

Left – The wedding of George Rix and Hilda Smith at Tilbury in 1926. Second row, from right, are John Smith, Laurie and Walter Murphy. Seated, from right, is Mrs Jane Smith and bridesmaid, young Laurie Murphy. (45) Below – Catherine Winder sitting outside West Lodge at Swanmore Park in 1930. (46)

just three years, her husband died of tuberculosis. Kathleen then lived once again with her mother at Swanmore Park and for some years worked in the laundry. It soon became apparent, however, that Kathleen had contracted tuberculosis from her husband. In the early 1930s she was admitted to a sanatorium at Chandlers Ford and was to remain there for some ten years. Catherine meanwhile continued to serve as cook at Swanmore Park till her death in 1946.

Another person to figure in the Murphys' life during these years was Laurie's sister, Hilda. In the early 1920s Hilda went to work as cook in a house at Sittingbourne in Kent. One of the other servants had a brother who would occasionally pay them a visit. His name was George Rix, a quiet reserved man who worked for the Port of London Authority. Hilda and George were married in 1926 and made their home at Tilbury. They had two children, Reggie and Eileen, and during the late 1930s they spent several enjoyable summer holidays in the Candover Valley.

*

The interwar years witnessed several changes amongst the local landowners. In 1920 Mrs Hope left Preston House and moved down to the Grange where she remained until her death in 1936. Preston House was occupied, in fairly swift succession, by Sir Cecil Burney, Admiral of the Fleet; Oswald Toynbee Falk, a wealthy man of the City and a notable economist; and Edward Kenward, a brewer. In 1933 the estate was acquired by another brewer, Colonel Miles Courage. Wilfred Buckley meanwhile remained in occupation of the Moundsmere Estate until his death in 1933. Two years later his widow sold it to a merchant banker named Herman Andreae.

There were some changes amongst the tradesmen too. The Allens' grocer's shop and bakehouse closed down, leaving the village with two general stores, the butcher's shop and *The Purefoy Arms*, plus *The*

Walter seated on his motor-cycle with his nephew Reggie Rix in about 1938. (47)

The Kenwards

Edward Kenward hailed from Sussex where his father Trayton Kenward was tenant of the Manor Farm at Icklesham. The family's fortunes were really founded during the 1850s when they took over a brewery in the village of Hadlow near Tonbridge. Their first venture ended in bankruptcy in 1868. Then Trayton, together with his brother Charles, a hop merchant, entered into partnership with John Court, a brewer who had previously worked for the London Brewery. The partnership flourished and by the 1880s the Hadlow brewery was employing 50 men and boys. It owned or leased 58 public houses and had an office in Tonbridge. In 1888 it went public as Kenward & Court.

Edward was born in 1877, the fifth son in a family of eight and, on completing his education, he joined the family brewery. In 1903 he married Muriel, the daughter of Major General Henry Haywood of the 45th Regiment Sherwood Foresters who lived at Belvedere in Kent. Edward and Muriel lived for some years at Bexleyheath but during the 1920s they decided to purchase a country estate.

This decision reflected Edward's keen interest in country sports, an interest which first brought him to the Candover Valley in the early 1920s when he purchased a shooting box called Axford Lodge on the Nutley Manor Estate. He was thus well placed to purchase the Preston House Estate when it came up for sale in 1927.

He went on make more acquisitions, including land at Southwood and Nutley Manor which, together with some smaller additions, increased the size of the Preston House Estate to nearly 3000 acres. His sporting interests were well served by the woodlands which were included in these acquisitions, and he hosted some very lavish shooting parties over the following years. He also kept three hunters.

Preston House itself was kept fully staffed and extensively redecorated. Part of the stable block was converted into garages, one for four large cars with its own servicing pit, and one for two small cars.

The Kenwards' lavish lifestyle was made possible by Edward's considerable investment income. Then, in the autumn of 1929, there occurred the "Hatry Crash", a notorious City scandal involving one Clarence Hatry, a City financier, who tried to overcome his financial troubles by manipulating share prices and making fraudulent issues of municipal stocks. Edward was one of many investors who lost heav-

Edward and Muriel Kenward (48)

ily when Hatry's group of companies finally collapsed in bankruptcy.

For a time the Kenwards held on at Preston House hoping matters would improve. Then, to cut down on their expenditure, they took up the tenancy of Preston Manor Farm from Major Herbert Aris and went to live in the farmhouse. Their hopes were finally dashed in the financial crisis of August 1931. The house and estate were put up for auction the following June. Preston House and Home Farm were eventually bought by Colonel Courage. The Kenwards retained Nutley Manor for another two years, residing during that time at Axford Lodge. They then sold that estate to Colonel Courage as well and moved to Tenterden in Kent.

In 1945 Kenward & Court were taken over by Charles Hammerton & Co. Ltd. The Hadlow brewery continued to function for a few more years with Edward serving as Chairman, before it finally closed down in 1949. Muriel died in 1954, Edward five years later.

Edward and Muriel had one son, Peter, who was born in 1908. He pursued a military career in the 14th/20th hussars and was a very keen equestrian. It was through this interest that he met Betty Kemp-Welch who would later become famous as the author of the social column "Jennifer's Diary". Peter and Betty were married in 1932. He left the army and worked for his father at Kenward & Court, in due course becoming Managing Director. He had one son by Betty but the marriage was not a success and they were eventually divorced in 1943. He subsequently remarried and had three more sons. He died in 1977.

*Left – General Hope, taking the salute at the unveiling of the war memorial in 1920. **(49)**
Below – The Reverend Thomas Walton and his wife. Ordained in 1901, he served as curate of Holy Trinity Church, Winchester from 1909-17. He then became vicar at Preston, following the death of the Reverend Sumner Wilson, and remained till 1947. **(50)***

Crown at Axford. The carpenter and wheelwright continued in business while building work was now largely handled by Harry Whitworth, a craftsman plumber, whose son Reg later took over the business. The Hall brothers' cycle shop evolved, as in so many other villages, into a taxi business and a car repair workshop, with petrol sold in two gallon cans. The premises were taken over in 1926 by Tom Nobbs, who extended the workshop and had petrol pumps installed. Pratts, Shell and Ethyl were amongst the brands of petrol sold, together with paraffin and eventually calor gas.

Preston acquired its own village hall in 1919 – a former army hut, erected opposite the school on land belonging to Preston House. Some public tennis courts were subsequently laid out on the adjoining field. Further down the road near the pond, a memorial was erected in honour of the 15 men of the parish killed in action during the war. The house and barns belonging to the Croft were later demolished and replaced by a substantial detached house, while the

*Below – The pupils of Preston Candover school with their teacher, Miss Winifred Seymour, in 1928. **(51)***

The Nobbs Family

Tom Nobbs in 1966 (52)

Henry Thomas Nobbs (usually referred to as Tom or Nobby) was born in 1898 at Cattistock near Dorchester where his father was the tenant of Higher Chalmington Farm. Tom was brought up to work on the farm and, as a consequence, became an accomplished horseman. Thus, when the time came for him to serve in the First World War, he joined his local Mounted Division, the Dorset Yeomanry, with whom he served in Egypt and Palestine.

On returning home, he went back to work on the farm and it was there, while out riding one day, that he came to the attention of Hilda Amy Loud. Her parents ran a hotel, *The White Horse*, at Cattistock where Hilda was recuperating after an illness. She and Tom were married in 1921 and were to have three children – Denis, John and Barbara.

Tom and Hilda started their married life on a small farm at Burton Bradstock near Bridport. This venture coincided with the onset of the farming depression and by 1926 Tom was ready to give up the struggle. In searching for a new line of work, he spotted a sale notice in the local paper for a motor repair business at Preston Candover. Tom had never had any formal training in motor vehicle maintenance but he had gained some experience of lorries and engines during his wartime service. He also had an extremely enterprising nature. He thus travelled up to Preston Candover, took a look at the premises and decided to go into the motor trade.

The Nobbs were to be an integral part of life in Preston for the next 25 years. During the war years Tom served as a Special Constable and the contact point for Army HQ and the Home Guard. He also served on the Parish Council and was captain of the village cricket team. Both Tom and Hilda were leading members of the village tennis club and took acting roles in the Shakespearean dramas performed by the Candover Players in the late 1920s.

The family left Preston in October 1949. Tom worked briefly as a chauffeur at Northington Grange. He then bought a filling station on the main London-Brighton road at Crawley in Sussex. Though it was a highly profitable business, the location was clearly going to suffer from the imminent expansion of Gatwick Airport, so he decided to sell up and in 1952 took over a filling station at Copythorne near Cadnam. This turned out to be a far less lucrative venture. Tom considered looking for a new garage property but he then noticed an advertisement for a caravan park at Bashley near New Milton. This he duly purchased in 1954 and ran it for the rest of his working life.

Tom died in 1974, Hilda the following year.

Above – Tom with Hilda. (53)
Right – Barbara. (54)

The tennis courts opposite the school, with the Nobbs' motorcycle being ridden by Jean Snow and John Nobbs. (55)

Left – A charabanc outing from Preston Candover in 1924. (56) Below – The Savill family's Rolls Royce, together with their chauffeur, Gilbert Sheail. (57)

pond was filled in and grassed over. Apart from that, however, the village saw relatively few changes in its appearance during these years.

Even so, the lives and outlook of its inhabitants were to change a very great deal. This was due in part to developments in mechanical road transport. For, whilst car production had ceased in Britain during the First World War, huge numbers of lorries had been built for service in France and further afield, and thousands of men had become familiar with driving and maintaining motor vehicles. Jack Chivers, the carrier at Preston, was just one of thousands of tradesmen who in the early 1920s disposed of his horses and invested in motor transport – at first a Ford van and then a lorry.

Steam-powered vehicles continued to be employed for certain tasks. In the early 1930s the meadows at Brown Candover were excavated for gravel and the Preston blacksmith was called on to repair a Foden steam wagon used for hauling out the gravel. All through the 1920s, however, steam fought a losing battle with oil in the powering of road vehicles and during the 1930s traction engines and steam wagons largely disappeared.

The Preston gentry all acquired cars during the 1920s. So too did many of the farmers and tradesmen, while some of the shopkeepers invested in a delivery van. Such developments quickly broke down the former isolation of country life – for exam-

ple, people in the Candover Valley could now receive their daily newspapers on the day of publication. They also had more flexibility in the provision of services. The village lost its resident physician in 1914 when Doctor Gauge went off to serve at the Front, and the parish was thereafter served by a practice in Alresford. Surgeries were held in a room at the Forge Cottage and were attended by a doctor who travelled out from Alresford, at first by motorcycle and later by car.

A major component of this change was the motor coach. The first bus service to be provided in the valley began in 1925, operated by Tom Perry of Winchester. This was succeeded in the late 1920s by the Venture Bus Company operating from Basingstoke. Preston's motor proprietor, Tom Nobbs, bought a succession of coaches during the interwar years. With these he provided a school bus service – a very necessary service after the catchment area of the Preston school was extended in 1927 to include Brown and Chilton Candover and Northington. Tom also provided a special bus service to Basingstoke each Wednesday and Saturday. The village butcher would sometimes put a basket of meat on board which Tom would deliver as he passed through Axford, Nutley, Farleigh and Cliddesden. He also ran a service to

A Morgan three-wheeler, owned by relations of the Colbys of Upper Farm, Bradley. (58)

29

Alton market on Tuesdays and often carried live poultry and calves on board the bus.

In addition to shopping trips, the motor bus also catered for sports and entertainment. A charabanc provided by Watsons of Basingstoke was regularly hired during the summer months for outings to the seaside or the races. Tom Nobbs provided a Saturday evening bus service to Basingstoke for people who wanted a night out at the cinema. He was also very keen on cricket and was made captain of the village team, partly because he owned the means for transporting the players to the away matches.

A colourful event of the late 1920s was the founding of the Candover Players. This came about through the enterprise of the Headmaster, Edward Harman, working in partnership with the Reverend Edward Gough, the Vicar at Chilton Candover. Their productions of *Macbeth* and *Hamlet* earned them considerable acclaim in the locality, but their success was also due to the fact that large groups of people could now be conveyed cheaply and easily by motor coach from the surrounding district.

With the increased use of motor transport came changes to the public roads. In the early 1900s the roads of the Candover Valley were macadamised with flint. The stones were gathered from off the fields, hammered into fragments, and then pressed into the roadbed with a steamroller. Over time the

The people of Preston Candover enjoying a day out at Bournemouth in 1923. Laurie Murphy and her young daughter are sitting at the front, second and third from the right. **(59)**

surface would become rutted by the iron-clad wheels of the carts, while the centre of the road would be broken up by the horses' hooves. Motor vehicles not only added to the wear of the road surface but they threw up clouds of dust in their wake. Many experiments were undertaken by the County Councils to overcome the dust problem and during the 1930s the country roads were gradually upgraded and capped by a layer of bitumen. Most of the gravel dug out of the pits at Brown Candover was used in this work.

The Candover Players. Above – Some of the cast of Hamlet. *From left, George Westbrook (farmer), Sid Rolfe (groom) as Hamlet, Tom Nobbs (motor proprietor) and Jim Colby (farmer).* **(60)** *Left – The cast of* Macbeth. **(61)**

A Girl Guide camp at Burton Bradstock on the Dorset Coast in the early 1930s, attended by some of the girls of the Preston Candover troop. Back row, from left: Jean Snow and Joan Westbrook; front row, from left: Ruth Smeeth and Rosemary Westbrook. Back row, third from left is the troop's Guider, Mary Walton, the Vicar's daughter. (62)

The Murphys were one of the few families in the village who took no direct role in the Candover Players, since they considered themselves to be totally lacking in acting skills. Nonetheless, they were always keen to join in the various village activities, whether that be the WI or the Brownies, and to take part in social occasions. They particularly enjoyed the whist drives which in the 1930s were held every week at the village hall. Prizes normally consisted of household goods and crockery, obtained by Reginald Harrison, the Headmaster, at wholesale prices, but at Christmas they would also include pheasants, cake or wine contributed by the gentry. Laurie could play a very mean hand when it came to whist and one year between September and Christmas she won a prize nearly every week.

Unfortunately, Walter still had a yen to be "one of the lads" and this could sometimes lead him into acts of total irresponsibility. He always wanted to be part of any drinking session and, if this occurred at the end of the week, he would have to borrow from Laurie which left her very short in her household budget. Worse still, with his weak stomach, such drinking sessions would always lay him low for several days. The most memorable act of irresponsibility occurred at the Silver Jubilee celebrations of 1935. Walter launched the celebrations in style by "firing the anvil". Then later that night, egged on by the patrons of

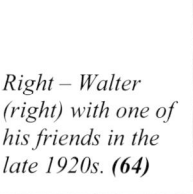

Left – General Hope supervising the unearthing of a ancient burial urn in Longbarrow Field, Lower Farm in 1935. Walter stands just behind him, one of several villagers who came along to join in the excavation. (63)

Right – Walter (right) with one of his friends in the late 1920s. (64)

Scenes from the pageant staged by the children of Preston Candover for the Silver Jubilee celebrations of 1935. (65/66)

31

The Rowe Family

The Rowes made up one branch of a huge extended family who had dwelt at the far western tip of Cornwall for several generations. They made their living primarily from farming.

Philip Rowe was born in 1858 and was brought up on his family's 60 acre farm called Tresowas, at Germoe near Helston. In 1881 he married his mother's cousin, Mary Tyack, who lived on Venton Vedna Farm, a holding of similar size to Tresowas, in the neighbouring village of Sithney. Philip was very ambitious and an extremely tough individual – he once had one of his farm workers horsewhipped. He was also a fierce disciplinarian to his family who in time came to number six boys and five girls.

During the first 16 years or so of their married life, Philip and Mary remained in Cornwall. They lived firstly at St Clement near Truro, then moved back to Sithney where Philip's cattle all died from anthrax. Then during the 1890s word spread that good opportunities for farmers existed in Eastern England. For there, landowners were positively seeking tenants from Ireland, Wales and the West Country, since they reckoned men from such areas would work harder than the local breed of farmer. Mary's brother moved up to Much Hadham in Hertfordshire in the early 1890s and Philip eventually decided to follow suit. They lived first at Walkern Park Farm near Stevenage. Then in 1901 they moved to Roe End Farm at Markyate near Dunstable.

By this time, with his older sons now in their teens, Philip was able to expand his farming enterprise. Over the following years the family moved three times, remaining on each farm for a few years, then moving on with one of the sons left behind to manage it. In time Philip came to hold Roe End Farm at Markyate, Coombe Grove at Gamlingay in Cambridgeshire, and Roby's and Manor Farm at Brown Candover in Hampshire with, at one time, his son Gerald in charge at Roe End, Clement at Coombe Grove, and George at Roby's.

Philip's principal line of business was cattle rearing, and for this purpose he bought a farm at East Huish near Tedburn St Mary in Devon to act as a gathering point for the cattle he acquired in the West Country. His eldest son, Philip Richard, was placed in charge of that farm. Then in 1929 Philip bought Ritson Barton Farm at Halwell, near Totnes, which he placed in the hands of his youngest son, Herbert.

Philip and Mary Rowe and their family in about 1897. Their last child, Herbert, was born the following year. **(67)**

Ritson Barton Farm became the home of Philip and Mary in their final years. Mary died in 1931 after a long illness, during which time she was nursed by one Daisy Whitehead, the district nurse for Strete. Daisy and Herbert were married in 1932. Of his five daughters, Philip allowed only the second girl, Hilda, to marry and that was because her choice of spouse was a Methodist Minister. The other daughters – Mary, Dora, Irene and Gwen – were required to remain at home and help with running the farm.

Philip died suddenly in January 1941 while staying at Roby's Farm. In subsequent years his descendents would continue to run the farms at East Huish and Roe End. During the war years Herbert left Ritson Barton and took on a succession of farms in the locality, but his efforts were finally frustrated when the land was taken over by the Government for a Battle Training Area. For a while he turned to agricultural contracting. Then in 1946 Daisy persuaded him to give up farming altogether and go into the seaside hotel and boarding house business. They duly took up a guest house at Salcombe and continued in this line of business throughout the 1950s while their sons went on to pursue academic careers in science and engineering. Herbert died in 1987, Daisy a couple of years later.

George Rowe remained a bachelor and after his father's death, he continued to live at Roby's Farm, together with his four spinster sisters. He had always found farming a tedious business, however, and in 1943 he gave up the tenancy of the farm. In subsequent years he moved down to Devon and made a living breeding racehorses. He then returned to Hampshire and bought a house in Andover, where he lived out the remainder of his days in considerable comfort, his sisters taking care of his every need. He died in 1969.

*Right – The Forge Cottage in the 1930s. At the gate stand Katherine Padwick and her daughter-in-law, Flo. Just to the right can be seen part of an extension which Alan Padwick built on the end of the cottage in the 1920s to accommodate his family. Thereafter his parents lived at the left hand end of the cottage. (68)
Below – William Padwick and Walter Murphy at work in the smithy in about 1920. (69)*

the beer tent, he carried out a second unscheduled firing at just after midnight. The furore that followed was so unrelenting that he vowed never to fire an anvil again – a vow he steadfastly maintained for the next 33 years.

*

Walter's relations with his uncle became increasingly strained during the 1920s. This was due in great part to the general sense of insecurity which came to pervade the blacksmith's trade. Walter, like many other smiths, wanted to explore the potential for new lines of work. William Padwick, however, preferred to stick his head firmly in the sand and try to survive by spending the absolute minimum on the business. Then in the spring of 1928 he suffered a severe bout of illness. Over the following months he lost all interest in the business and went off to stay with a friend at West End near Southampton, leaving Walter to run the smithy single handed. For a time he contemplated selling up and moving to West End permanently, but in the end he returned to the Forge Cottage where he died of cerebral thrombosis in February 1929. His estate was worth £741.

Ownership of the business passed to his widow while Walter carried on as the sole employee. Although Aunt Katherine in turn kept a tight rein on expenditure, Walter did now have more freedom to pursue his own ideas. During the 1930s he built up a very solid reputation for the quality of his work and for his reliability. He mixed with fellow smiths in the National Master Farriers' and Blacksmiths' Association, attending their annual dinner and outing. He began entering the local farm shows organised by the Alresford and District Agricultural Society. His motorcycle, though originally bought for pleasure outings, soon became an integral part of the business for, with his tools and equipment carried in the sidecar, he was able to range further and travel faster than was previously possible.

The smithy itself saw few changes during the interwar years, partly because, in the absence of mains electricity, there was little scope to upgrade the equipment. The major exception to this was oxyacetylene welding. The traditional welding technique employed at the smithy was relatively limited in its application. It could not be employed, for instance, to repair a crack in the casting on a farm implement. In other cases the smith had to spend time dismantling and then reassembling the implement, just to isolate the broken part. Also, since many farm implements were left outdoors, the nuts and bolts would usually be thick with rust. And the traditional method was of no help when farmers started wanting their implements converted from horse to tractor-drawn. The best William Padwick could do was patch together a drawbar using iron plates and rivets.

In the late 19th century an alternative welding technique had become available. It involved the mixing of acetylene gas with oxygen to produce a very hot flame and during the 1900s it came to be widely

Above – Walter (with his elbow on a lifebelt) and Laurie sitting on a pleasure boat at Marlow, during the annual outing of the National Master Farriers' and Blacksmiths' Association, 1938. Charlie Padwick stands bare-headed at the right hand end of the very back row, next to the two men in trilbies. In the front row, second from right, stands Bill Pearson, the Bradley blacksmith. (70) Right – Walter outside the smithy in 1934, using his oxy-acetylene welding kit to cut and shut an iron tyre. His daughter Laurie looks on. (71)

adopted in the shipbuilding and engineering industries. With the development of road haulage in the 1920s, it became feasible for gas cylinders to be distributed beyond the industrial centres to country towns and even to more remote country districts. Walter first heard of the technique in the late 1920s from a relative, Charlie Padwick, the blacksmith at Bishop's Sutton. Then in the spring of 1930, about a year after William's death, Walter received an invitation from the British Oxygen Company (BOC) to attend a welding demonstration at a smithy in Basingstoke. About 10 blacksmiths from the Basingstoke district attended the demonstration. Of those, only Walter and one other showed any interest.

Walter eventually managed to convince his Aunt Katherine that the £10 required for the kit would represent a worthwhile investment and so the purchase went ahead. The only training he received in its use was a brief lesson from the BOC rep who delivered it. Otherwise he had to try and acquire the necessary skills as he went along, aided by a 1928 edition of a *Handbook for Oxy-Acetylene Welders*, given to him by Charlie Padwick. He found, as did many other blacksmiths, that oxy-acetylene welding was nothing like so easy as it appeared. If he paused too long with the flame, a hole would suddenly appear in the metal. If he was too hasty, the parent metal would not be sufficiently melted. A weld might often look sound but it would subsequently turn out to be weak and brittle. Nonetheless, he persevered.

He undertook his first welding job in May 1930. His annual consumption of oxygen and acetylene then grew to around 3000 cubic feet per year and, apart from 1935, remained at that level for much of the decade (Graph 4).

Oxy-acetylene welding had applications in all aspects of the business apart from shoeing, and in several of these areas it proved far more efficient than traditional methods. In converting implements from horse to tractor-drawn, Walter could now fabricate drawbars which were far neater and more robust than before. In the case of wheel-binding, the tyre no longer had to be manhandled from the fire to the anvil and back, which meant that Walter could single-handedly make new tyres and cut and shut existing ones. Also, whereas previously the surplus lengths of tyre had been wasted, Walter could now weld these together to make a whole new tyre. Cracks and breakages in farm implements could often be repaired with the part still in situ. If some dismantling was required, then a blast from the blowpipe would soon free any rust-hardened nuts. Welding also helped bring in custom from beyond the parish. For, whilst farmers continued to use their local smiths for shoeing and other traditional tasks, they now brought the more specialised jobs over to the Preston smithy.

*

Despite such enterprise, the interwar years were to be a generally lean time for the Preston blacksmith. Prices had risen steadily following the outbreak of war in 1914 and had carried on rising throughout the war and the post-war economic boom. When the boom finally collapsed in the winter of 1920-21, prices had tumbled for several months before settling at around a third of the pre-war figure. They remained at that level throughout the 1920s, then dipped even lower during the years of the Great Depression. Then in the mid-1930s the economy began to recover and as a consequence, inflation started to edge upwards.

There is unfortunately a gap in the accounts of the Preston Candover smithy from 1914-25 and so a detailed record of the business is only available from 1926 onwards. Graph 1 shows the blacksmith's income in both actual figures and at 1970 prices. Thus, when wartime inflation is taken into account, it is clear that the business could not command the same level of income in the interwar years as it had done before 1914. In real terms, annual income declined by 25% between 1910-26 and by 38% between 1910-39. The high point was 1935 when work was exceptionally plentiful. The low point was 1938, though this was largely due to Walter being laid up for much of February and March, following an operation for appendicitis.

William Padwick and Walter Murphy outside the smithy in the early 1920s (72)

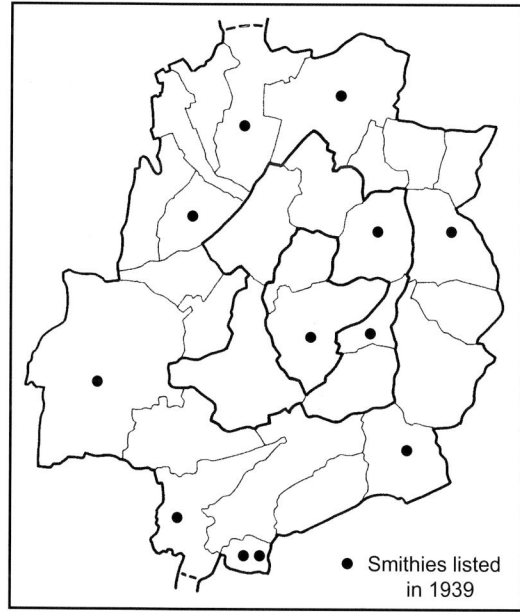

This decline in the blacksmith's income occurred despite the fact that he was drawing a greater proportion of his work from further afield than hitherto, owing to the closure of other smithies in the district. For whereas in 1907 there had been 23 blacksmiths located in the area shown on the map above, this figure had fallen to 16 by 1931 and to 12 by 1939. In the case of those parishes adjacent to Preston Candover, the smithy at Bradley was still in business in 1939, those at Brown Candover and Dummer had closed down, and a new one had been established at Ellisfield.

During the late 1920s about 90% of the Preston blacksmith's income was still derived from customers with properties in Preston and Nutley. This figure dropped markedly after 1930 (Graph 2) – to 70% in 1933 and 65% in 1939. The change resulted mainly from the acquisition of a major new customer, Walter Henry Savill, who took over Chilton Manor Farm in 1927, and from those farmers in Brown Candover who moved their accounts to Preston after the local smithy closed down in about 1931.

During the interwar years the type of customer dealt with by the Preston blacksmith was much the same as in 1910, apart from the tradesmen. The income derived from the latter group declined between 1914-26, partly because most of them had dispensed with their horses but also because they no longer undertook farming as a sideline. Some income was generated by new enterprises established in the locality such as the motor repair garage at Preston, and the Pioneer Poultry Manure Company – set up in the late 1930s in the former smithy at Brown Candover, taking in manure from the poultry farms in the district and processing it into a powdered fertiliser.

The proportion of the blacksmith's income derived from the different types of work was also remarkably similar to that of 1910 (Graph 3). Shoeing and related work continued to be the dominant activity. Farm-related work was a relatively minor activity until the late 1930s. All the other categories of work provided a modest source of income, only showing a slight increase when some special development took place in the locality – such as when a registered slaughterhouse was built at Poasley in 1930 and Walter was called on to provide the fittings, or when the gravel pits were excavated at Brown Candover and he was engaged to service the excavating and washing machinery.

*

Between 1910-14 the income earned by the Preston blacksmith from horseshoeing amounted to 64% of the total. Between 1926-39 the figure was virtually the same. Nonetheless, there were some fundamental changes in shoeing work over the period.

The Farm Tractor

British farmers remained generally indifferent to the tractor until the onset of the food crisis of 1917. By then huge numbers of men and horses had been diverted to the needs of the military. In its efforts to increase food production, the Government turned to the United States for help, and by November 1918 some 6000 Fordson Model F tractors had been imported into the country. American manufacturers were to dominate the scene in the interwar years – Allis-Chalmers, Case, International Harvester, John Deere, Massey-Harris, but especially Fordson whose famous Fordson Standard was first produced at their Dagenham plant in 1933.

These tractors were relatively cheap – a Fordson Standard cost about £150, the equivalent of three horses. They were generally limited to towing implements from a drawbar. Some types were equipped with a pulley by which they could drive barn machinery – an innovation which rapidly led to the demise of the steam threshing contractor. Many also came equipped with "power takeoff" which allowed direct transmission from the tractor's engine to the implement mounted or drawn at the rear. None of the models, however, made any concession to driver comfort and they could easily rear over backwards if the implement hitched behind encountered an obstruction.

A particular drawback of the early tractor was its wheels. Throughout the interwar period tractor designers tried to devise driving wheels smooth enough to allow the tractor to be driven on the public roads without damaging the surface but with sufficient traction to pull implements on wet soil. Various solutions were tried but none proved really satisfactory. A common method was for the iron tyre to be fitted with cleats or spade lugs. It was not until the late 1930s that the problem was solved by the application of the low pressure pneumatic tyre. Even then, the changeover to pneumatic tyres took several years to complete – Walter Murphy fitted his last iron tyre to a tractor in 1952. In the meantime the tractor was effectively confined to the land and in these circumstances the horse still had a useful role to play.

The introduction of a tractor onto a farm required careful consideration as to how the work was to be allocated between tractor and horses, since it was impractical for implements to be made interchangeable between the two. In general, the tractor was seen as ideal for heavy work and especially for ploughing, or for steady continuous operations such as grass cutting and harvesting. Horses could then be kept for light work such as harrowing and for carting crops and materials about the farm.

In the early 1920s many farmers simply hitched the horse-plough to the tractor but this was very inefficient since it required a second man to guide the plough in the traditional manner. The problem was soon overcome by the introduction of the "tractor plough" which could be attached directly to the rear of the tractor. It was also provided with a self-lift mechanism by which the driver could lift the plough out of the ground for transport or for manoeuvring on headlands. Such innovations demonstrated the potential for further farm mechanisation, but this was thwarted for much of the interwar period by the farming depression.

Farm workers took up tractor driving with minimal training and accidents were therefore quite common. Ploughing by tractor also called for a totally different approach to the traditional method. Even so, the lessons were soon learnt and the farm worker became increasingly dissatisfied with having to tend the farm horses. For, although tractors needed regular maintenance, they did not require daily watering, feeding and grooming.

By 1926 the prices charged for shoeing had increased since 1914 in line with inflation. The pricing system had also been changed, so as to accord with the system recommended by the Farriers' Association which set down a scale of prices for different sizes of shoe. During the late 1920s most workhorses were charged for at 8/6d a set, hunters at 8/-. In the early 1930s, however, some of the farmers negotiated a lower price for shoeing their workhorses, a move which may have been triggered by the economic depression and the fall in wholesale prices. In 1934 the pricing system was simplified and all workhorse shoes were then charged for at 8/- a set. This lasted until 1937 when, following a growth in the rate of inflation, the price was increased to 9/-.

NATIONAL MASTER FARRIERS' ASSOCIATION
(Winchester & District)
List of recommended charges on & after April 1st 1918

Feet measuring:	Per set:
4½ inches & under	4/6d
5	5/-
5½	5/6d
6	6/6d
6½	7/-
7	8/-
7½	8/6d
8	9/6d

Private Ponies 6/-   Carriage Horses & Hunters 7/-
Shoes removed & roughing – Half the price of new shoes
Unruly horses, & horses requiring special attention, charged for accordingly
Extra charge for journeys

Bringing in the harvest between the wars.
Left – By traditional horse-drawn wagon at Manor Farm, Preston Candover. (73)
Below – By tractor on one of the farms at Preston Candover in 1938. (74)

Graphs 5 and 6 show how the number of horses shod each year, and the number of shoes made and fitted, declined during the "missing years" in the smithy accounts between 1914-26. In percentage terms, however, the decline in the number of shoes was greater than in the number of horses. The graphs also show that the number of farm workhorses shod remained fairly constant until the end of the 1930s, but that the number of shoes made for these horses declined steadily from 1932 onwards. It appears, therefore, that during these years the horses came to be shod much less frequently than in 1910-14.

The reasons for this varied over the period. In the early 1920s it was caused mainly by the replacement of the tradesmen's horse-drawn vans with lorries and light motor vans, and the gentry's carriages with cars. This meant that horses were used far less for haulage work on the roads.

The farm tractor only began to make an impact during the 1930s. Westbrook Brothers at Home Farm were amongst the first farmers in Preston Candover to acquire an oil-powered tractor. They did so at the behest of the youngest brother, Percy, who had acquired considerable engineering skills while serving on the Western Front. Fordson tractors also appeared on the land at Lower Farm and at Moundsmere during the 1920s. Walter happened to be shoeing at Moundsmere Farm when the tractor was delivered. Most of the farmhands went to watch it being demonstrated, but the old carter who was with him in the stables, declined to do so, saying he would see enough of it before the day was out. And indeed that evening he was called on to take out a team of horses and drag the tractor from where it had been driven deep into a hedge.

On the whole, however, the number of tractors acquired by local farmers seems to have been fairly modest. Amongst the farm customers of the Preston blacksmith, only three out of 14 customers in 1926 had work done which related to tractors or tractor ploughs. By 1932 the figure was six out of 19 farm customers and this kind of ratio endured for much of the decade. Nonetheless, with the introduction of tractors, the farm workhorses could be used for much lighter work than hitherto and this reduced the frequency with which they needed to be shod.

Thus by 1939 the annual production of horseshoes at the Preston smithy was about 38% of the annual average for 1910-14. This was one reason why, after William Padwick's death in 1929, the business could be handled by one man.

The types of horses kept by the gentry varied over the period. During the first part of 1931 Peter Kenward kept a team of four racehorses at the Preston House stables. In 1934-35 Colonel Courage fielded a team of polo ponies. These created a great deal of work for the blacksmith, for the team comprised eight ponies and during April-August they had to be shod every two weeks. Walter often shod at least three ponies at a session and on one day in July 1934 he shod a total of six.

The number of hunters kept by the gentry was fairly modest during the 1920s. They belonged principally to Edward Kenward and to Mrs Hope and her son, General John Hope, at Preston Grange. The situation changed radically, however, with the arrival of Colonel Courage and Herman Andreae. Both men developed stables sufficient for hunting on five consecutive days on a rota system. Some eight hunters were kept at the Preston House stables but there was

Sheaves being brought to the rick by horse-drawn wagon at Upper Farm, Bradley. (75)

37

The Aris Family

Herbert Aris was born in 1868 at Lois Weedon in Northamptonshire. Though his family were of farming stock, Herbert chose to follow a career in teaching. He was educated at Rossall School in Lancashire and at King's College, Cambridge. He later returned to Rossall where he served as Assistant Master from 1894-1905. He then took up a post at Winchester College. From 1908-18 he served as the Commanding Officer of the College's Officers' Training Corps. He also became a House Master in 1911.

Then in 1915, at the age of 47, he abandoned his bachelor status. His bride was Sydney Dorothy Arundel. Her father, John Thomas Arundel, had spent many years in the South Pacific, establishing coconut plantations and prospecting for guano. In 1882 he returned briefly to England where he married Eliza Whibley, the daughter of a Bristol silk mercer. Their elder daughter Lillian was born a couple of years later in New Zealand. Sydney Dorothy followed in 1885, being named after her birthplace, Sydney Island in the Phoenix Group.

Eliza died back in England in 1887. Lillian and Sydney Dorothy were thereafter brought up by their Whibley grandparents and aunts, while John continued to prosper from his involvement in the coir, copra and phosphate industries of the Pacific. In 1909 Lillian and Sydney Dorothy, having completed their education, joined him in the Pacific and went on a tour of the islands, but the voyage was dogged by accidents and ended with the ship being wrecked on a reef near Tahiti. John thereupon resigned from the company and retired to England, where he lived at the Savoy Hotel in Bournemouth until his death in 1919.

The following year Herbert resigned from Winchester College and he and Sydney Dorothy came to live at South Hall in Preston Candover where he subsequently purchased the nearby Manor Farm. They had two children, John and Elizabeth. Herbert became a JP in 1926. He also served as Honorary Secretary to the Parochial Church Council at Preston and was an enthusiastic supporter of the festival choir.

Also, from 1921-30 he was a Member of the Council of the Central Landowners' Association, a body which sought to protect the interests of owners of agricultural and rural land in England and Wales.

In the early 1930s the family left Preston and went to live in the New Forest at Northerwood House near Lyndhurst. There Herbert

Herbert and Sydney Dorothy Aris. (76)

immersed himself in New Forest affairs. He served on the Verderers' Court and was made Chairman of the New Forest Town and Country Planning Committee as well as Chairman of the Fenwick Cottage Hospital at Lyndhurst. In 1935 he became a Governor of University College, Southampton whilst in 1940 he was picked as High Sheriff for Hampshire.

After the war Herbert decided to give Northerwood House to the nation, to be used by the Forestry Commission, and returned to South Hall where he died in 1952. Sydney Dorothy moved to London and died there in 1966.

Their son John went to King's College, Cambridge in 1935 and then briefly to McGill University. During the war he served in the Canadian Army and rose to the rank of major, after which he joined the British Council, for whom he worked until his retirement in 1977. He died in 1989.

Their daughter Elizabeth meanwhile remained single and, after Herbert's death, took over the running of Manor Farm. She also became a member of the Parish Council in 1950 and served as Chairman from 1955-64. She finally sold up the farm in 1970 and moved to Wiltshire where she lived until her death in 2000.

John and Elizabeth Aris. (77)

Left – Elizabeth Aris being given riding tuition by the groom at South Hall in the late 1920s. (78) Below – Farmer Jim Colby with his daughter Joan (standing beside him) and the Westbrook children Joan, Rosemary and Michael at Upper Farm, Bradley in the 1930s. (79)

also considerable turnover in numbers – a total of 18 hunters was accommodated between 1933-38. At Moundsmere Manor Herman Andreae kept a stable of about seven animals. Thus in 1938, of the total shoes made at the Preston smithy, 44% were for hunters.

There was incidentally a marked contrast between the names given to hunters and workhorses. The hunters were given such exotic names as Sir Kingsley, Swiftsure, Dorset, Jackdaw Moon, Big Dixon, Kangaroo and Wallflower. Farm workhorses were generally given names like Blossom, Damsel, Prince, Flower, Tommie, Trooper, Diamond, Colonel, Dumpling and Kitt. On one occasion Herman Andreae acquired a hunter named Kitt but this name was eventually changed to Nell Gwynn. Only one horse, a pony first shod for Wilfred Buckley in 1912, was given the name Dobbin.

Throughout the interwar years the making and fitting of new shoes brought in about 94% of the total income earned from horse-related work. Of the remaining 6%, the bulk of the work comprised removes. Other types of activity varied a good deal. In January 1927, in the aftermath of the great blizzard which fell on Christmas Night, there was a high demand for rough-nailing – between 20-22 January the smith rough-nailed a total of 24 horses. The increase in the number of hunters led to a greater demand for light hunter plates. And, as before, the blacksmith was occasionally called on to attend a lame horse, though now the veterinary surgeon would sometimes be in attendance.

*

Throughout the interwar years the estates of Preston and Nutley were divided between seven main farms. The Hopes retained ownership of Lower Farm which they let to a tenant. Colonel Courage did the same

Tom Nobbs taking part in a pageant at Moundsmere in the 1930s. The horse was borrowed from Mr Frank Halliday. He lived at Box Cottage near North Hall and kept two hunters throughout the interwar years. (80)

with the Home and Nutley Manor Farms. Most of the other landowners exercised direct control over their farms with the day-to-day management being handled by a bailiff or manager.

The farmers of the Candover Valley responded to the depressed state of agriculture in different ways. Poultry farming enjoyed a vogue in the 1920s and several smallholdings in the district were taken over for this purpose, but most of them went out of business after a few years. The exception was the Bradley Egg Farm. It was founded in the early 1920s by Harold Bliss, who had previously worked as an accountant in East London. He developed it into the

The Burtons

Frank Burton came from Wiltshire where his father was tenant of a 40 acre farm at Monkton Deverill. Born in 1858, Frank carried on running the family farm after his father died. In 1886 he married Mary Ann Burleton, whose family ran the New Inn, plus a mill and a 200 acre farm, at Monkton Deverill. They lived for a time at Warminster before taking up Prospect Farm at Monxton near Andover. Then in 1901 they came to Lower Farm at Preston Candover. Their family eventually comprised seven sons – Burleton (known as Jack), Theodore, James, Frank junior, Sidney, Albert (who died in infancy) and Septimus.

Jack left home in his early twenties and worked on various farms in the district. He eventually wound up at the farm of John Poulter at South Warnborough where in 1915 he married John's daughter Eliza. The following year he returned to Preston and took over Lower Farm in his own right, while his parents moved to the Grange Farm at Old Basing. Jack and Eliza were to have two girls and one boy.

In the early 1920s Lower Farm came to house Jack and Eliza and their three young children, plus his brothers Frank junior and Sidney. It was at this time that Jack was reported to the village constable by Ruth Mills, a former house servant, for swearing at her out in the road. He was duly charged under a county bylaw relating to the use of indecent language in a public place, and appeared at a Court of Summary Jurisdiction in Basingstoke in April 1921. Though he was acquitted, it later emerged that, in giving evidence, Jack had committed perjury, and for that offence he received three months hard labour.

Christopher Burton with his bride, Audrey Hedderley, on their wedding day in 1943. (81)

The disgrace of Jack's imprisonment broke up the family. Frank junior went to live in Basingstoke where he worked on the local farms. He died of tuberculosis in 1923. Sidney married Ruth Mills, the servant girl at the centre of the court case, in 1924 and, together with his brothers Theodore and James, emigrated to Canada. The youngest brother Septimus went to live with Frank senior at the Grange Farm. He carried on there after his parents died and did so successfully until his death in 1981.

As for Jack, he carried on at Lower Farm till 1927, then moved to Breach Farm at Dummer. The farming depression, however, finally pushed him into bankruptcy and in the mid-1930s the family moved to a bungalow at Oakley where he found work as a farm labourer. Eliza died there in 1945, Jack in 1949.

Their son Christopher broke away from the family's farming tradition, becoming an apprentice at Thornycrofts in Basingstoke in 1935. After wartime service in the navy, he joined Wallis and Steevens and enjoyed a very successful career as a farm machinery salesman until his retirement in 1983.

---

largest egg farm in the country. It employed 52 people, had a total stock of more than 25,000 birds, and an annual output of 4.5 million eggs.

The traditional farm economy of the valley finally collapsed as huge volumes of New Zealand lamb were off-loaded onto the home market. Westbrook Brothers at Home Farm were just one of many farmers who sold off their flock of Hampshire Downs sheep in the late 1920s. They concentrated thereafter on arable farming, employing a rotation of wheat, barley, oats and rye, plus a catch crop of clover or sanfoin. This was supplemented by a dairy herd of 12 milking cows, from which they supplied milk to the village.

Several other farmers took up cattle farming and dairying during the interwar years and by the mid-1930s about half the farmland in Preston and Nutley consisted of permanent pasture. Wilfred Buckley had disposed of his pigs and poultry during the war and thereafter concentrated on dairying. Philip Rowe, the tenant of Roby's Farm at Brown Candover, was primarily a cattle farmer and held several farms in different parts of southern England. John Ritchie Hamilton was primarily a cattle dealer, but he also made a practice of taking over pieces of unwanted land and using them for raising stock. In 1927 he took over Moth Farm at Brown Candover. It comprised 320 acres and at that time had a very poor reputation. The meadowland he turned over to gravel extraction. The remainder he put down to grass, bought in all the hay, cereals and other food he needed, and in this way raised a large head of cattle.

During the 1930s Rex Paterson, a close friend of Hamilton's, arrived in the district. He had commenced farming on his own account in the late 1920s on a holding of 80 acres near Winchester, which he ran as a dairying operation. To keep his costs to a minimum he employed a system developed by Arthur Hosier, a farmer at Wexcombe in Wiltshire. The system avoided tying up capital in permanent build-

The Farming Scene

During the First World War the farming community was very successful in increasing the production of cereals and potatoes, in part by ploughing up old grassland. Farmers had initially been reluctant to undertake such work, in case cereal prices fell to their low pre-war level. To allay these fears, the Government gave them guaranteed minimum prices for wheat and oats for the next five years. This brought prosperity to the land and in the immediate post-war period the Government agreed to retain the price guarantees.

There then began a world wide fall in prices. By May 1921 it was clear this fall would soon bring the guaranteed minimum prices into operation. At this, the Government hastily abandoned its commitment – an action thereafter known to farmers as the "Great Betrayal". The loss of Government support, plus the fall in wholesale prices, caused cropping plans to be abandoned, implements sold, and expenditure cut down on fertilisers, buildings and drainage. Much of the land ploughed up during the war reverted to pasture or was left to go derelict.

Successive Governments did little to assist the farming industry until 1931 when the Marketing Act was introduced with the aim of bringing stability to the market in milk and other food products. Subsidies were introduced whilst restrictions were instituted on food imports. As a result of these measures, plus the general upturn in the economy after 1937, agricultural production began to improve.

ings by using a portable "milking bail" which contained milking machinery and equipment. The bail was moved to a fresh plot of ground each day and in this way the cattle could dung the whole farm. By adopting this system, Paterson was able to develop a low cost dairying operation, well located in relation to the market for milk in London and the large south coast towns.

From these very modest beginnings Paterson's enterprise rapidly expanded, and came to be concentrated on the Hampshire downs where derelict farmland could be obtained at a very low rent. By 1939 his holding amounted to 7500 acres. His first acquisition in the Candover Valley was Moth Farm which he took over from Hamilton in 1936. He subsequently took over Swarraton Farm at Northington and Berrydown Farm at Ellisfield, which he used for the raising of young stock. The farming scene in the valley, therefore, came to encompass a major and somewhat unorthodox dairying enterprise.

The depressed state of farming during the inter-war years meant that, for the Preston blacksmith, only a relatively small proportion of his income was derived from servicing farm implements, carts and equipment – less than 10% in the years 1926-29 and 1930-34. The income derived from the different types of farm work remained broadly the same as in 1912. A significant change, however, occurred in the late 1930s. In 1937 such work brought in 21% of income and of that, nearly 80% was earned from work involving farm implements, as against 60% in 1912.

The type of implements dealt with was broadly the same as in 1912 – mainly those required for ploughing and cultivating, and for haymaking. Amongst the traditional implements, however, there had now appeared the disc harrow. Though introduced into Britain from America at the end of the 19th century, the disc harrow had a heavy draught and did not really come into its own until the advent of tractor power. By 1939 at least four of the blacksmith's customers had acquired a set. However, most of the growth in farm income in the late 1930s was probably due to the increase in the number of tractors in the locality, which in turn brought about an increased demand for implements and wagons to be converted from horse to tractor-drawn.

*

The Bradley Egg Farm in 1936. The crawler tractor was employed for carting food and water to the various units of the farm. The buildings behind were used for grading and packing the eggs. (82)

41

Above – Grass mowing at Upper Farm, Bradley in the 1930s. (83) Right – Lower Farm at Preston Candover. The wagon was originally horse-drawn, but was at some stage fitted with a tractor drawbar by the blacksmith. (84)

The technological changes which occurred during the interwar years did not have a wholly negative impact on the Preston blacksmith's livelihood, especially since he had taken up oxy-acetylene welding. In fact, the conversion of farm machinery was just one of several new lines of work. Another was the servicing of road mending equipment. By the early 1930s the Highway Board was becoming more mechanised and, as the tarmacking of the public roads proceeded, so their need for the blacksmith's services changed. In 1927 the maintenance of pickaxes for the Board, as a proportion of tools income, stood at 13%. This fell to 5% in 1932. By 1936 the Board had ceased bringing hand tools to the smithy, but it did occasionally call on Walter to service its roadmaking implements, tar barrels and sprayers, and steamrollers.

Not all tractor owners needed to call on the blacksmith for tractor-related tasks. Wilfred Buckley, for instance, employed his own blacksmith and plumber and also a fitter to maintain the engines and generators on the Moundsmere Estate. But where farmers did make use of the local blacksmith, the work often involved making adaptations to seats and drawbars and repairing such items as mudguards, gear levers, oil pipes and radiators. Prior to the introduction of pneumatic tyres, Walter repaired and replaced the iron tyres and also fabricated the spade lugs (which he nicknamed "spuds").

From time to time Walter was also called on by Tom Nobbs to help out with the car repairs at the garage – perhaps to weld the odd spring, silencer, exhaust pipe or brake handle. He also made adaptations to Tom's buses, putting in new steps and fittings for extra seats.

However, the actual income derived from these areas of work was very small. In 1937 Walter's earnings from horseshoeing brought in £167.9s.6d whereas his earnings from work involving motor vehicles and tractors amounted in total to £3.19s.8d – 64% as against 2% of the total income for that year. In no way, therefore, could the new lines of work compensate for the decline in the farriery side of the business.

Traditional and modern modes of transport outside Holdaway's Store at Preston Candover in 1920. The car belonged to Wilfred Buckley. (85)

War & Austerity

Walter marked the outbreak of the Second World War with another act of blithe irresponsibility. He decided to acquire a dog, a black labrador puppy which he brought home one day after doing a shoeing job at Moundsmere Farm. At the time, of course, Laurie was still getting to grips with food rationing and she was less than happy at being presented with an addition to the family. The dog grew rapidly and, since he had unusually large paws, he was given the name Jumbo.

Walter had owned dogs in the past and always fancied himself as a natural dog handler. The trouble was he could never resist spoiling them – Jumbo, for instance, was the sole recipient of the Murphys' chocolate ration all through the war. As a consequence the dogs never obeyed Walter's commands unless it suited them and, if he should become especially tiresome, they would sink their teeth into him with complete impunity.

Jumbo was just one of a host of complications which affected the Murphy household during the war years. Their home was now one half of a small thatched dwelling called Church View Cottage which stood next to the village green. They had moved there from their previous cottage at Preston Manor Farm in the mid-1930s. Church View Cottage was much closer to both the centre of the village and the smithy. Its main drawback was that for six weeks of the year it would be inundated by the spring floodwaters. During that time the family would live on boards laid across brick piles and wait for the waters to subside, after which it would take several months for the cottage to dry out completely.

The Rix family were much in evidence during the early years of the war. Hilda and her two children, Reggie and Eileen, were holidaying at Preston when war broke out, so overnight they acquired the status of evacuees. They did not return home to Tilbury until the following March. Then, when the bombing intensified in the autumn of 1940, they came back to Preston and remained there till May 1942. Thus, during that time, the Murphys' little two bedroom cottage was often called upon to accommodate up to six people.

Above – No. 4 (Preston Candover) Platoon, "C" Company, 3rd (Basingstoke) Battalion of the Home Guard at the Minden Day Parade in July 1944. Front row, 9th from left, is the Commanding Officer, Charles Elbourne, the manager at Preston Manor Farm. On his right sits the Second-in-Command, Theodore Balding, tenant at Nutley Manor Farm from 1933-45. Front row, far left, sits Corporal Bill Pearson, the blacksmith at Bradley. Private Walter Murphy stands in the back row, 6th from left. (86)
Right – Walter and Jumbo outside the smithy, some time in the 1940s. (87)

The Savills

The fortunes of the Savill family were founded in the 1850s by Walter Savill. His father ran a substantial building company in Chigwell, Essex. There were five sons in the family. The eldest took over the family business, while the others went into brewing, stockbroking and – in Walter's case – shipbroking.

Walter first worked as a clerk for merchants Willis Gann & Co. Then in 1858 a fellow clerk, Robert Shaw, had a disagreement with Willis Gann which led to his salary being cut. Shaw promptly quit. Walter soon followed and together they formed their own shipping company. In 1882 they merged with the Albion Company to form Shaw Savill & Albion. The company was to comprise other shipping companies and at one time it had a close association with the White Star Line. It specialised in the New Zealand trade, carrying emigrants and manufactures on the outward voyage and bringing back frozen meat.

In 1864 Walter married Matilda Burness, the daughter of a provisions merchant. They lived initially at Chigwell, then moved to Hove in Sussex where they raised a family of five girls and five boys. In the early 1900s Walter moved to a house at Lindfield, near Haywards Heath where he died in 1911.

His eldest son, Walter Henry, was born in 1867 and educated at Charterhouse before going into the family business. He was to spend many years in the City, becoming a ship-owner and a Director of several companies, particularly those concerned with shipping, tea and rubber. In 1905 he married May Marriott. They had one child, Kenneth, who was born in 1906. The family lived initially in London but then in 1916 Walter, now divorced, moved to the Manor House at Upton Grey in Hampshire. He remarried and continued to live at Upton Grey till 1936.

Walter Henry Savill with his second wife Christine, at the Manor House, Upton Grey. (88)

In 1924 the Manor Farm at Chilton Candover was put up for sale by auction. It was bought initially by John Ritchie Hamilton, but he then sold it to Walter Henry Savill in 1927. Some ten years later work began on the building of a manor house at Chilton on the hillside above the farm. It was completed shortly before the outbreak of war.

Walter Henry was very interested in farming and country sports. In his younger days he had been a keen rider to hounds but this interest was abruptly curtailed when a railway accident left him with a permanent spinal injury. He maintained his interest in horses, however, particularly in the racing field and was the owner of several successful racehorses. Shooting was also a favourite pursuit and he became a knowledgeable collector of sporting pictures. His interests in country matters also encompassed education and he served as a Trustee and Manager of the school at Preston Candover. He died in 1953.

His son, Kenneth, was educated at Winchester College. He made his career in the army, progressing from Sandhurst to the 12th Royal Lancers and then the King's Dragoon Guards. In 1935 he married Jacqueline Salusbury-Hughes, whose family lived at Offley Place near Hitchin in Hertfordshire and whose father was a brigadier with the Grenadier Guards. They had three daughters.

During the Second World War Kenneth served in France, North Africa and Italy. During this time he briefly took command of the Green Howards and soon afterwards was invited to rejoin the 12th Royal Lancers as their Commanding Officer. In 1947 he joined the Queen's Bays, was appointed to the rank of Colonel in 1950 and retired some four years later. A number of honorary appointments followed in subsequent years, including that of Gentleman-at-Arms in Her Majesty's Bodyguard and Colonel of the Queen's Dragoon Guards. He was also appointed High Sheriff of Hampshire in 1961 and Deputy Lieutenant in 1965.

Kenneth Savill as a Lieutenant in the 12th Royal Lancers (89)

Walter's daughter Laurie, after a brief spell as a trainee nurse at Andover Hospital, went into domestic service. She first worked as a housemaid for Emily Anderson at Fawkners, then became cook for the Savill family at the newly constructed manor house at Chilton Candover. There she met Fred Sheail, the son of the Savills' chauffeur and soon to be a Private in the Hampshire Regiment. They were married at St Mary's in Preston Candover in February 1941 and eventually set up home some 15 miles away at Church Crookham. In due course they presented the Murphys with two grandsons, John and Philip. After the war Fred became a telephone engineer with the GPO.

Relations between Walter and his Aunt Katherine had often been strained during the 1930s but they now became positively stormy. This was partly because Katherine refused to increase his wages in line with wartime inflation, but also because Walter felt he was effectively running the business and should therefore have complete control over it. She in turn was quite prepared to rid herself of the responsibility but he, of course, had no capital with which to acquire it. They finally took the matter to a Basingstoke solicitor and, on his recommendation, they drew up an agreement whereby Katherine would lease the business and premises to Walter for a period of 50 years. The agreement was signed in July 1943.

For some years Katherine had lived at one end of the Forge Cottage, the other end being occupied by her son Alan and his family. In 1947 she suffered a bad fall and as a consequence moved in with Alan's family. By then Walter was anxious to move out of the flood-prone Church View Cottage, so Alan agreed to let him have the vacated end of the Forge Cottage. As part of the agreement, the Murphys were obliged to continue with an existing arrangement whereby the room at the front of the cottage was made available twice a week for holding the doctor's surgery. Walter was thus able to return to his boyhood home, right next door to the smithy. Katherine meanwhile took to her bed and stayed there till her death in 1951.

The Murphy and Rix families at Preston Candover in 1940 with, back row, Laurie, George and Hilda, then young Laurie, Eileen & Reggie (with Jumbo). (90)

*

With the outbreak of war in September 1939, the citizens of Preston Candover, as elsewhere, were at once drawn into supporting the war effort. The Headmaster, Reginald Harrison, was already serving as billeting officer. Preston formed part of a recep-

Left – Walter and Laurie outside St Mary's Church at Preston Candover on the occasion of their daughter Laurie's wedding to Fred Sheail in February 1941. (91)   Above – The groom with five of his six sisters. (92)

The Colbys

The Colby family hailed from the village of Bletchingdon near Oxford. Head of the family was James Colby, a shoemaker by trade. During the 1840s he and his wife Ann raised a family of three boys and one girl. The eldest son Charles followed in his father's trade while the others went into domestic service.

During the 1870s the second son, James Bond Colby, served as butler to Lord Viscount Hereford at Tregoyd in the Welsh borderland. At some stage over the following years his circumstances brought him to Preston Candover where he served as butler to the owner of North Hall. One evening he was, apparently, in attendance on the owner and his guests at table. The talk over dinner was much concerned with the forthcoming Derby and one of the guests proffered the name of a sure-fire winner. James promptly went into town and put all his savings on that particular horse. It duly won.

Though he was now in his late forties, James decided that, with this sudden upturn in his fortunes, he would give up domestic service and start a wholly new life as a farmer. In 1895 he took up the tenancy of the

James Colby, his wife Alice and son Jim at Manor Farm, Preston Candover in about 1910. (93)

nearby Preston Manor Farm. In April of the following year he married a servant girl of 28 named Alice Rudderham. They were to have one son, Jim, who was born in 1898.

The family remained at Manor Farm till 1911, whereupon they moved to Upper Farm at Bradley. Jim became a very keen horseman and it was while out riding one day in about 1918 that he first met his future wife, Kathleen Wilson. Her family came from Kirk Langley in Derbyshire, where her father had been a farmer. In the 1900s he brought the family south to Hampshire where he became agent for Lord Jeffreys at Burkham.

Jim and Kathleen were married in 1920. They had one daughter. James Bond Colby died at Upper Farm in 1930, Alice in 1953. Jim then carried on running the farm until he retired in 1968. He died in 1974.

Jim and Kathleen Colby at Upper Farm, Bradley in the 1930s. (94)

tion area designated to receive evacuees from Portsmouth and a few days after war was declared, some 30 children arrived in the village.

Tom Nobbs, the garage proprietor, was made a Special Constable and became the contact point for air raid warnings and orders to the Home Guard from Army HQ. Alan Padwick was made the Senior ARP Warden while two of the building tradesmen, Fred Earwicker and Reg Whitworth, helped run Preston's Fire Service. Another 40 men of the parish served in Preston's Home Guard platoon. Their HQ was located in the former hunter stables at Preston House while their observation post was sited on the high down near Moundsmere.

Walter joined the Home Guard. He responded immediately to the call for Local Defence Volunteers in May 1940 and, since he owned a motorcycle, he was made Company dispatch rider – a dubious honour, as it turned out, since he was constantly in danger of being shot at by every platoon in the valley. On the other hand, it did mean he was issued with a Lee Enfield rifle before any of the other volunteers and on occasions he was called on to lead large and impressive army convoys across country. His glory days as a dispatch rider finally came to an end on the advice of his doctor, who told him that motorcycling was aggravating his susceptibility to colds and chills. With great reluctance, therefore, Walter sold off the

Vellocette and bought a second hand car, initially an Austin 7 and then an Austin 10.

The war came to touch upon several other aspects of life in the valley. Four miles to the east of Preston an area of land just north of Lasham village came into use as a Mosquito bomber station. Four miles to the south stood Northington Grange which became the centre of a huge storage area for military equipment and later served as HQ for the 47th U.S. infantry division. Thereafter, groups of GIs became a frequent sight, their vehicles parked all over the district, and an object of intense interest to the local children. Within the parish the mansion at Moundsmere was taken over as a military hospital.

The valley witnessed the odd moment of excitement and alarm. There was the night when a fighter plane crashed close to Moundsmere Manor, and "Battle of Britain Sunday" when some children set fire to a rick and the villagers had to labour all afternoon to put out the blaze before nightfall. Quite a few bombs and landmines fell upon the downs. Once or twice the bombers appeared to be seeking an actual target, usually the searchlights at Candover or Wield, but more often they were simply jettisoning their unused bombs before heading back to base. Such incidents were particularly prevalent during the time of the Coventry raids in November 1940. However, no-one was hurt as a result.

There were several false alarms over mysterious flashing lights, parachutists and Fifth Columnists but, once the threat of invasion had passed, life in the valley came in many ways to be little affected by the war. As everywhere, rationing became a major preoccupation. Its effect was mitigated to some extent, since most families grew their own vegetables and kept chickens and in some cases a pig as well, and in the summer months it was usually possible to secure a rabbit.

Since farm work was a reserved occupation, there were relatively few families with fathers or sons in the armed forces. At the end of the war just three

Private Walter Murphy, dispatch rider, outside Church View Cottage in 1940. (95)

names were added to the war memorial on the green, in contrast to those of the 15 men who had fallen in the war of 1914-18. There was relatively little friction between village children and evacuees, most of whom settled in well. Life thus came to revolve around haymaking and harvest and around such social activities as cricket and football matches, fetes, flower shows and whist drives – though these activities would often be directed towards such causes as raising funds for Spitfires or for "War Weapons Week".

*

It was in his role as a country blacksmith that Walter was to make his most meaningful contribution to the war effort. For the wartime food campaign could only meet its objectives through the increased use of farm machinery, and it was imperative that this machinery be kept in working order. The person best

The Preston Candover cricket team in the mid-1940s. (96)

The Hamiltons

John Ritchie Hamilton spent his formative years in Scotland and the north of England. He was born in 1877 in Carnwath near Lanark, the second son of William and Jane Hamilton whose family eventually came to number six sons and two daughters. They moved down to Cumbria in about 1882 and settled in the village of Cotehill near Carlisle. William was a brick and tile maker. In time he became manager of the brick works at Cotehill with his son James serving as foreman. Of his other sons, Thomas and Alexander became joiners while John and young William became butchers.

One of the Hamiltons' neighbours was William Little, a farmer at High Cotehill. The Little family comprised seven children, of whom five were girls. Three of the girls became very attached to the Hamilton boys and a succession of weddings duly took place – Mary to Thomas, Clara to James, and Margaret to John. The latter's wedding took place in Edinburgh in November 1904. He and Margaret were to have one child, Jean, who was born in 1910.

During the early 1900s John's involvement in the butcher's trade appears to have encompassed livestock dealing and he also dabbled in the dairy trade as well. At some stage he seems to have concluded that his fortunes would fare much better in the south of England and so he moved his family, together with his parents, down to Surrey and to a holding called Stilehurst Farm in the village of Capel near Dorking. Some of his brothers subsequently came south too – James to a farm at Farley Mount near Winchester and William to Stocks Farm near Droxford.

For John's wife and daughter, Stilehurst Farm was to be the first of many moves between different farms over the next 30 years. John's habit was to take over some stretch of unwanted land, fence it in and put stock on to grass, then after a few years move on to a new holding. His farms came to include Lower Breach Farm at Ockley in Surrey and New Zealand Farm at Upper Chute in Wiltshire. He took over Moth Farm at Brown Candover in 1927. Both New Zealand Farm and Moth Farm were subsequently handed on to Rex Paterson. Alongside his farming activities, John dealt extensively in livestock, especially cattle. He also ran a brickworks at Warnham near Horsham and, while at Moth Farm, he extracted the gravel deposits alongside the Candover Brook.

Also during his time at Moth Farm, John employed a young worker named Nelson Dance whose family had farmed Cowdown

John Ritchie Hamilton with his wife Margaret and daughter Jean at Stilehurst Farm near Dorking in about 1913. (97)

Farm at Clatford. Nelson married the Hamiltons' daughter Jean at Brown Candover in June 1932. They were to have two daughters. In 1937 Nelson took over Finkley Manor Farm near Andover and was to remain there till his death in 2005.

On giving up Moth Farm in 1936, John moved to Manor Farm at Whitchurch. He died there in March 1941 at the age of 64 and was buried at Brown Candover. Margaret went to live with Jean and Nelson at Finkley Manor where she died in 1955. She was buried next to John at Brown Candover.

John Hamilton was a very well known figure in farming circles throughout much of Hampshire, Wiltshire, Surrey and Sussex, particularly in the sale yard, to which he would be driven by Jean in an old black car. A quiet gentle man, he was an extremely shrewd judge of people as well as being a natural salesman. He was also possessed of a very generous nature. Rex Paterson was just one of many people he helped, either through his extensive knowledge of the local farming scene or through putting them in the way of suitable land or livestock. He seems to have been a very poor organiser and never kept any proper records of his numerous transactions. Even so, his stock nearly always did well and showed a profit, and when he died in 1941 his estate was worth some £24,500.

*The green and garage at Preston Candover in the late 1940s. Above – Tom Nobbs' 20-seater Bedford bus. **(98)** Right – Tom's taxi, a Ford Mercury. Walter continued to do jobs for the garage but, as in pre-war years, it made only a minor contribution to his income. **(99)***

placed to fulfill this role was the country blacksmith, but it was unclear how many smiths had the skills necessary for really complex engineering work.

The body most concerned with this issue was the Rural Industries Bureau (RIB). It had come into being in 1921 with the aim of fostering rural crafts and activities. A major part of its work related to the country blacksmith, to whom it proffered advice on craft skills, modern manufacturing methods, design and business advice. As the country moved closer to war, the RIB concentrated on supporting the expansion in home food production which it could do most effectively by assisting blacksmiths in the repair of farm machinery. In 1940 the RIB carried out a survey of smiths to ascertain the range of skills and equipment available. It then drew up a scheme of high quality training to help those men who needed to improve their skills. The scheme was initially targeted at some 900 selected smiths. The RIB also set up a Rural Industries Equipment Loan Fund to assist those craftsmen engaged in repairing agricultural machinery to obtain equipment on easy terms.

Walter was included in the RIB survey of 1940. A major problem encountered by the RIB during the interwar years was simply reaching the people they most wanted to help, and Walter for one had been unaware of their existence. From now on, however, he enjoyed a long and fruitful association with the Bureau, making use of their Equipment Loan Fund and their training courses.

The latter was recommended to Walter by the RIB representative who could see that his self-taught skills in welding would be greatly enhanced with some expert tuition. Over the next two years the RIB's trainer visited the smithy every couple of weeks, bringing test pieces for him to work on. These would involve different types of machinery or different types of metal, whether steel, malleable or cast iron, brass or copper. He was also taught different welding techniques.

The most difficult part of the course was pre-heat welding. This technique was required in cases where the item to be repaired would expand and contract during the welding process and, if this was not properly taken into account, it would affect the quality of the weld. This was particularly important in complex castings. The training course required him to weld a crack in an engine block, for which he had to place the block on the forge, encase it within a furnace made of firebricks, fill the furnace with charcoal, heat it till the block was red hot, and then perform the welding operation.

The course proved a most challenging experience, particularly as he had to fit it in alongside his normal work, his Home Guard duties, and his often complex domestic arrangements. Nonetheless, he finally succeeded in obtaining his Certificate of Worthiness in welding in December 1942.

Walter's consumption of oxygen and acetylene gas increased considerably during the war years (Graph 4). He first employed pre-heat welding as part of his work in May 1942 and used it occasionally in the repair of castings on tractors, plough wheels, rollers and elevators. Far more use was made of a technique called "bronze welding". Strictly speaking, this was a soldering, not a welding, process since it involved bonding metals together by the use of a non-ferrous alloy such as manganese bronze. It could be used in the repair of items ranging from motor car wings and panels to cast iron articles and to machine parts made of copper, brass,

Charlie Padwick

Charlie Padwick's father came from the hamlet of Armsworth near Old Alresford. Although a blacksmith by trade, he ran a pub at Bighton for a few years after his marriage in 1867. He then settled down as the blacksmith at Bishop's Sutton.

Charlie, born in 1872, eventually took over the business. In the 1920s he responded to the decline in horseshoeing by specialising in ornamental ironwork and in time earned himself a countrywide reputation. He took a close interest in the work of the National Master Farriers' and Blacksmiths' Association, right from its inception in 1907 when he became Secretary of the Winchester Branch. He was also an organiser for the Guild of Hampshire Craftsmen and held a high position in the Rural Industries Bureau.

A regular church goer, he was for many years a churchwarden and bellringer, a Sunday School superintendent, and a member of the Parochial Church Council. He was also a keen gardener and beekeeper. He died in 1949.

During the interwar years he became much admired in the smithy trade for his example, sympathy and helpfulness to other blacksmiths in the district. Walter Murphy was one who benefited greatly from his advice, particularly in taking up oxy-acetylene welding.

Charlie Padwick (back row, far left) with the Alresford and District Agricultural Show Committee in about 1930. (100)

---

bronze, galvanised iron, and certain alloy steels. A major advantage of bronze welding was that it often avoided the need for pre-heating the machine part and thereby the need for extensive dismantling. Thus, as his training progressed, Walter used bronze welding for repairs to tractor wheels and bearings, pumps, grass cutters, milking machines, and car engine components.

The other major innovation of the war years was the installation of electric power in the smithy. Preston Candover was connected to the mains just on the outbreak of war and Walter immediately applied to the Mid-Southern Utility Company for a power supply to the smithy. This was turned down because the current was only sufficient to provide lighting. At first Walter made the best of the situation, but by 1943 he was finding it impossible to meet his customers' needs with the antiquated equipment at his disposal. His prime concern was to replace the hand-driven bellows with an electric blower and, since the rating of a blower was about the same as a vacuum cleaner, he reckoned it could be run satisfactorily off the light fitting. The old bellows were thus replaced and dumped, without regret, behind the pigsties in the meadow.

These makeshift arrangements were eventually discovered by an inspector from the company. Walter was at first threatened with prosecution but, after due negotiation, he made a fresh application and three power points were then laid on – one for the blower, the other two for an electric drill and a grinder which he bought through the RIB's Loan Fund.

*

Once again, the outbreak of war was followed by a rapid increase in prices, which this time the Government sought to control through rationing, subsidised and controlled food prices, and other measures. These controls were retained in the early post-war years, so as to avoid the kind of economic slump which had occurred in 1921. Thus the economic climate of the 1940s was to be very different from the interwar years when prices generally remained stable or even fell slightly.

Graph 1 shows the blacksmith's annual income in both actual figures and at 1970 prices. The 1930s ended on an unremarkable note, with income in 1939 standing at £271. Although income increased between 1939-41, it did not keep pace with the rate of inflation. Thus it was not until 1942 that income started to grow in real terms. Thereafter, this growth was quite spectacular. The peak year occurred in 1944 when the business earned £622. Income then fluctuated between £600-£635 throughout the late 1940s. This meant that from 1944 onwards the business was able to command a level of income which, in real terms, was higher than that of 1910.

The income derived from customers living (or responsible for properties) outside Preston Candover and Nutley increased markedly in the early 1940s, particularly in the adjacent parishes (Graph 2). This increase was largely brought about by the farming activities of Rex Paterson. Moth Farm at Brown Candover now generated far more work for the Preston smithy than in the pre-war period. Paterson also sent work to the smithy from his farms at Northington and Farleigh, and on occasion from those at Oakley, Micheldever and Stockbridge.

Above – The closing meet of the Hampshire Hunt at Moundsmere in April 1946. (101) Right – A family group at Moundsmere. From left, John Nitch-Smith, Sophie Shone, Joy Andreae, Michael Shone, Herman A. Andreae (Master of the Hampshire Hunt), and Herman K. (Sonny) Andreae. Sonny and Sophie were Herman's children by his first marriage. John Nitch-Smith was Joy's son by her first marriage. He later farmed College Farm at Ellisfield. (102)

The 1940s saw a fundamental change in the type of work undertaken at the smithy (Graph 3). Throughout the interwar period, despite the general contraction in the blacksmith's income, horseshoeing had remained the predominant activity and still comprised 63% of total income in 1935-39. This figure fell steadily during the 1940s while a corresponding growth occurred in farm-related work. 1944 was the year when the business first earned more from farm work than from shoeing. The other categories remained generally the same as a proportion of total income, apart from construction-related work which showed a significant increase in 1945-49.

*

Throughout the 1940s Walter continued to charge a flat rate for shoeing workhorses and hunters but, owing to wartime and post-war inflation, the price charged had to be constantly revised upwards.

The amount of shoeing work undertaken by the Preston blacksmith increased during the early years of the war. This was due in part to the petrol shortage which meant that, although farm machinery was now employed on an unprecedented scale, workhorses still had a useful role to play – Rex Paterson, for example, employed horses to collect milk from the milking bails and cart it to the farmstead. Much of the increase, however, was due to the activities of George Rowe who lived at Roby's Farm in Brown Candover. He was especially interested in horses and, alone amongst the blacksmith's customers, his stock of farm animals included three mules. The number of horses kept at Roby's Farm rose from 10 in 1939 to 16 in 1941, but eight of the horses which the farm acquired during 1941-42 were only shod once or twice. It is possible, therefore, that George went in for some horse dealing during these years.

At the national level, the number of workhorses declined rapidly once the war was over and, owing to the chronic meat shortage, many of these animals

| PRICES CHARGED FOR SHOEING 1937-49 ||
Date	Price per set
1937 (May)	9/-
1940 (January)	10/-
1941 (October)	11/-
1942 (January)	12/-
(October)	13/-
1944 (April)	14/-
1945 (January)	15/-
1946 (July)	16/-
1947 (July)	17/-
1948 (January)	18/-
1949 (January)	19/-
(November)	20/-

The Patersons

Rex Munro Paterson was born in 1902 and brought up in Wandsworth. His father was a clergyman, his mother the sister of the famous aircraft designer, Sir A.V. Roe. After attending Christ's Hospital School, he enrolled at Wye Agricultural College but soon left and worked on a farm near Ashford called Stowting Court.

After a few months, Rex developed a yen to go travelling in Canada and set sail in January 1919. He first worked on farms in Nova Scotia and Ontario and then on a cattle ranch in Saskatchewan, before taking up a small dairy farm in British Columbia. Owing to the world-wide collapse in food prices, he could make no headway with the farm and in 1925 decided to return to England.

He worked for a year back at Stowting Court but the English farming scene now seemed hopelessly complacent and inefficient. Early in 1927 he made plans to return to Canada but before doing so, he decided to make one final effort to find suitable farm employment in England.

He cycled through Surrey and into Hampshire, where he secured a job as a tractor driver. His mother thought this somewhat beneath him and offered to help set him up on a farm of his own. He thus took up the tenancy of an 80 acre farm in the Winchester district. Also, during his time at Stowting Court, he had become very attached to one of the dairy maids, Muriel Pantling, and they were married in October 1927. The couple ran the farm as a dairying operation, with a herd of 50 cows and a portable feed shed and bail. Rex had considerable skills as an engineer and these were used to good effect in his farming enterprise.

His Canadian experience had shown Rex how difficult it was to achieve viability on a small farm and he soon began to expand his enterprise. In this he was greatly assisted by the farmer and cattle dealer, John Ritchie Hamilton. They became close friends and over the years John not only furnished Rex with livestock but put him in the way of suitable farms. By the late 1930s the enterprise had come to be concentrated in the Hampshire downs and by 1942 his holdings totalled 10,000 acres, located in the Candover Valley and close to Oakley, Overton, Micheldever and Stockbridge. Hatch Warren Farm at Farleigh Wallop became the Patersons' home and headquarters for the whole operation.

All this made Rex a figure of some notoriety in the farming world. Not only was he a relatively young man but he came from a non-farming family and had no source of income outside farming. Yet, at a time of severe agricultural depression, he had built up a large scale farming enterprise and – most incredible of all – he claimed to be making a profit.

Rex Paterson (103)

The wartime food campaign gave Rex ample scope to pursue new methods and to employ his ingenuity in overcoming the crippling shortages of labour and materials. It also demonstrated the value of his record keeping system. His major problem was the antagonism he encountered from some members of the Hampshire War Agricultural Executive Committee. Rex resented having his methods questioned by people who had failed to make a profit from farming before the war. His attitude caused him to fall foul of the Committee in some minor instances and this gave his critics the opportunity to claim he was not obeying the cropping rules. The dispute achieved widespread publicity and became the subject of an official investigation. This eventually vindicated his claim that he was being victimised by local officials.

Muriel died in 1944. Rex remarried a few years later. In the post-war years he concentrated on dairy farming and continued to be a leading innovator, particularly in the development of ensilage methods and in the use of machinery. His best known inventions were the "buckrake" and the "fertispread", but the farm workshop also turned out a variety of scoops, pushers and scrapers.

Rex was one of the earliest farmer members of the British Grassland Society. He hosted the first National Grassland Demonstrations at Hatch Warren and presented several papers to the Society. He also conducted seminars at the Summer Meetings and in 1967-68 held the office of President.

He received many honours for his contribution to farming. He was made a Companion of the Institute of Agricultural Engineering. In 1964 he received the OBE and in the following year was presented with the Massey Ferguson Award for outstanding contribution to the advancement of farming in the UK. In 1970 he became one of the first people to receive a Fellowship of the Royal Agricultural Societies. He died in 1978.

The Farming Scene

As war approached in the late 1930s, so the farming community was once again called upon to maximise food production. Farmers, of course, were very mindful of the "Great Betrayal" and to allay their fears, the Government established guaranteed prices and markets for most staple products.

At the same time it established County War Agricultural Executive Committees and, below them, District Committees who were given extensive powers. They could take possession of unused land or idle machinery, give directions as to cultivation, management or use of agricultural land, and allocate labour, machinery, feeding stuffs and fertilisers. Their prime aim was to increase the area under grain and potatoes since this would provide far better food value than using the land to rear livestock, and thus each winter of the war saw the ploughing up of extensive areas of pasture.

Although the war years were marked by severe winters, the summers were generally fine and yielded record harvests. Greater prosperity led to an increase in the use of fertilisers and the adoption of new methods such as ley farming. More use was made of ensilage. The major change, however, was seen in the use of machinery, particularly following the establishment of Lend-Lease in 1941 when large quantities of farm machinery were shipped across the Atlantic. American implements soon began to find their way onto farms via a Goods and Services Scheme set up by the Ministry of Agriculture.

The war thus brought about considerable technological change in British farming, but doubts remained as to whether these achievements would be preserved after the war. In the event the Labour Government came forward with the Agricultural Act of 1947 which incorporated a system of guaranteed prices into the law of the country. Despite the austerity of the late 1940s, therefore, the wartime achievements of the farming industry looked set to continue.

This was evident, for example, in the development of the farm tractor. At first Fordsons continued to dominate the scene, especially when in 1945 they replaced the Standard with the Fordson Major. A year later, however, the Ferguson TE20 made its appearance and was an immediate success. It incorporated a three point rear linkage on which equipment could be mounted, all controlled by a hydraulic lifting mechanism. This greatly improved traction and safety, as well as opening up many possibilities for further mechanisation.

ended up on the butcher's slab. In the Candover Valley it would seem that both the number of horses shod and the number of horseshoes made and fitted remained fairly steady during the war years (Graphs 5 and 6). In 1944 the number of workhorses shod by the blacksmith stood at 54. Thereafter the numbers fell rapidly and by 1949 the figure was 23. However, only two farms had given up keeping horses altogether by that date – these being Home/Lower Farm and Preston Manor Farm, where the last horse was shod in June 1944 and August 1949 respectively.

The outbreak of war saw a reduction in the number of hunters shod by the Preston blacksmith, from 20 in 1939 to 12 during the middle years of the war. One huntsman, Frank Halliday, who lived in a cottage near North Hall, had kept two hunters throughout the interwar years, but he disposed of these before the start of the hunting season in 1939. Colonel Courage reduced his stable to one hunter in 1941 and finally gave up keeping horses altogether after June 1942. General Hope retained his two hunters at Preston Grange, though they were shod far less frequently than before. It was Herman Andreae who proved most successful at keeping his hunter stable in being during the war years. In 1939 his stable contained six horses. The numbers remained at about this level till 1943 when the total was increased to nine. Further acquisitions were made after June 1945 and thereafter the amount of activity at the stable returned to the pre-war level.

*

The Candover Valley saw nearly all of its permanent pasture put under the plough during the war years, including the bulk of the parkland above Preston House and the huge area of dereliction on Chilton Down. For some farmers the wartime controls were highly frustrating. Rex Paterson's unorthodox methods led him into a very acrimonious dispute with the Hampshire War Agricultural Executive Committee. Livestock farmers such as Harold Bliss, owner of the Bradley Egg Farm, had to close down their operation. On the other hand, wartime farming did offer considerable opportunities. Westbrook Brothers, for example, took over the holding of the Bradley Egg Farm. Having been occupied by free range poultry for some 20 years, the land produced record yields of grain which meant that, by the end of the war, the brothers had cleared their long standing overdraft and remained well in the black from then on.

With the introduction of crops such as potatoes and sugar beet, and with the advent of the Goods and Services Scheme, new types of implement began to appear in the valley, particularly after 1942. They included manure loaders and spreaders, potato ploughs and planters, combine drills (a drill which

New types of farm machinery being employed in Southern England in the 1940s. Above – A Thwaites green crop loader. (104) Left – A tractor-drawn Massey Harris combine harvester. (105)

distributed both seed and fertiliser in one operation), caterpillar ploughs, cabbage planters and green crop loaders.

The prime innovation of the war years was the combine harvester. Rex Paterson acquired a combine in 1941 and Herman Andreae had done so by 1944. These machines brought about a considerable saving in labour over the traditional binder since they could cut and thresh the grain in one operation. They did, however, require a pickup baler to collect the discarded straw and, although such balers were available, they were somewhat crude. The major problem was the need to dry the grain artificially before storing it. Drying and storage facilities were eventually set up on the Paterson and Andreae holdings, and also on a farm at Kempshott where they could be hired by other farmers in the district. Even so, the shortage of drying facilities remained a problem throughout the 1940s and acted as a brake on the further adoption of combines at that time. Certainly none of the farmers served by the Preston blacksmith was as yet ready to dispose of their binders.

Both the quantity and the increased employment of farm machinery generated an increased demand for servicing by the Preston blacksmith. Thus, whereas farm-related work had contributed 21% of total income in 1937, by 1944 this figure had risen to 37% and to 45% by 1949. The work was primarily concerned with the repair and servicing of farm implements. This reflected not only the increased use of implements, but also the need for existing machinery to be kept in a serviceable condition for far longer than would be necessary in peacetime. The impact of new types of implement was relatively small. Farm equipment also began to figure more in the work – in 1942, for example, Walter undertook a large amount of work relating to threshing machines, trussers and potato riddles.

Of particular importance in the Candover Valley was the development of implements for use in silage making. This came about through the activities of

A demonstration of a Paterson buckrake attached to a Ferguson tractor. (106)

54

Rex Paterson. With the lifting of wartime restrictions, Paterson could concentrate once more on dairy farming. In the post-war situation imported cattle feed was not the cheap option it had been in the 1930s and this, coupled with the increased demand for liquid milk, made ensilage a viable way of providing winter fodder. However, the harvesting, as well as the carting of the silage to the cattle, was very labour intensive. Thus in 1946 Paterson began experimenting with a type of hay sweep which could collect and lift the grass from behind the mower and place it directly in the pit or on the clamp. Walter was engaged to fabricate the sweep and also to convert the ex-military vehicle to which the prototype was attached. Following the introduction of the Ferguson tractor, Paterson designed an improved version of the rear-mounted sweep with hydraulic lifting gear. Then, having perfected the prototype, he sold the patent to Taskers of Andover. And, since he wanted to distinguish his invention from the traditional haysweep, he decided to use the American term for haysweep which was "buckrake". It was to prove a great success, both at home and abroad.

*

Although wheelbinding remained a minor part of the business during the 1940s, it did nonetheless undergo considerable change. In previous years the bulk of wheelbinding income had been earned from work involving farm carts and wagons. This was still the case in 1937 but during the 1940s a far greater proportion of the work involved farm implements and tractors. The traditional wheelbinding activities also declined during these years. Instead the work became primarily concerned with repairs to hubs, spokes and flanges – work which, with the increased use of all-metal wheels, was now more within the province of the blacksmith than the wheelwright.

Throughout the interwar years construction-related work had been a very minor part of the business. In 1937 it brought in only 4% of total income, but this proportion grew steadily to 10% in 1942 and 18% in 1947. The demands of war and post-war austerity caused a sharp reduction in the amount of work undertaken to the gentry's houses, stables and parkland and to their tied cottages. Instead, construction-related work came to be focused primarily on repairs, adaptations and new construction in farm buildings and other structures around the farmstead. This meant that Walter was now mainly called on to deal with items such as drains, water pipes, boilers and fittings for livestock pens. A notable area of work, especially in 1947, was fabricating the ironwork required for new farm gates. This could well represent the replacement of items sorely neglected during the depression of the interwar years.

CONSTRUCTION WORK 1937- 47			
	1937	1942	1947
Total income from construction-related work			
Actual income (to nearest £):	£11	£38	£111
At 1970 prices:	£34	£92	£263
The split between the different types of property served was:			
Gentlemen's residences	24%	5%	10%
Farmhouses & cottages	12%	6%	9%
Farmsteads	58%	60%	77%
Church & school property	6%	28%	3%
Other	-	1%	1%

Thus by the end of the war, the blacksmith's premises at Preston Candover had been effectively transformed from a country smithy into an engineering workshop, while its core business had changed from farriery to agricultural engineering – all of which was to stand Walter in very good stead amidst the farming prosperity of the post-war world.

WHEELBINDING WORK 1937- 47			
	1937	1942	1947
Total income from wheelbinding & related work			
Actual income (to nearest £):	£14	£17	£77
At 1970 prices:	£46	£40	£183
These sums were made up from servicing the wheels on:			
Farm carts & wagons	90%	43%	17%
Farm implements	1%	41%	24%
Tractors	4%	14%	57%
Other	5%	2%	2%
and from:			
Making & fitting new tyres	63%	36%	35%
Cutting & shutting existing tyres	30%	33%	20%
Other work	7%	31%	45%

Walter with his grandsons, John and Philip Sheail, and Jumbo at Church Crookham in 1947. The racing car was his own handiwork. (107)

The Westbrooks

The Westbrook brothers came to Preston Candover in 1912 when their father took up the tenancy of Home Farm. James Westbrook had been born at Droxford and had married Edith Bone, the daughter of a master bricklayer. For many years they lived at Corhampton Farm near Bishop's Waltham, where they raised a family of seven children – Mildred, Walter, Robert, Daisy, George, Madge and Percy.

The girls all married farmers or agricultural suppliers. Walter emigrated to Canada, George to Australia where during the First World War he served with the Australian Army (which included service at Gallipoli). At the end of the war he decided to return to England and join his father and his brothers, Rob and Percy, at Home Farm. James died in 1921 and the three brothers decided to carry on the tenancy as a joint venture, trading as Westbrook Brothers.

The depressed state of farming in the interwar years made life very difficult for the brothers, each of whom was married and had a young family. They were able to take over the tenancy of Lower Farm in 1936 which, together with Home Farm, gave them a total holding of nearly 800 acres. Also, on the death of James Westbrook, the children inherited the proceeds of a family trust which they agreed to maintain for the running of the farm and only take out their share of the annual interest. In this way, the brothers were able to weather the interwar years.

Rob was responsible for dealing with the workmen and the day-to-day management of tasks about the farm. George kept the accounts and ran the dairying side of the business. They kept 12 dairy cows for supplying the village.

The house and barns at Lower Farm, Preston Candover. Percy's family moved here from Home Farm in 1936. (108)

To deliver the milk, George converted a tricycle previously used for selling ice cream and on this he would cycle through the village, ladling out the milk into the jugs provided by his customers.

Percy had always been interested in machinery and had acquired considerable mechanical skills while serving on the Western Front. He therefore took charge of all the implements and equipment on the farm. It was at his insistence that the brothers acquired their first tractor in the early 1920s and that they finally gave up keeping workhorses in 1944. Even so, both Rob and George remained horsemen at heart.

Their farm holdings prospered during the Second World War and over the following years they were able to buy out the interests of their siblings in the family trust. Following the change of ownership at Preston House in 1961, they accepted a golden handshake to quit the tenancy of Home Farm. Rob, then in his 74th year, decided to retire and moved to Ropley where he died two years later. George and Percy carried on for a few more years at Lower Farm. Percy died in 1966, George in 1973.

The Westbrook brothers – from left: Percy, Rob and George (109)

Post-War Affluence

In the autumn of 1952 Walter's passion for wireless was ousted by a new piece of gadgetry – the television set. He was one of the first people in the village to buy a set. It stood proudly in the living room of the Forge Cottage, a neat cabinet of polished veneer with the screen tastefully enclosed behind a pair of doors. In later years his son-in-law, Fred Sheail, would convert it into a handy medicine chest. In the early days the reception in the valley was distinctly "snowy" but Walter still derived a great deal of enjoyment from his viewing and would carry on doing so over the next 30 years. His tastes were firmly middle-brow, encompassing the crime thrillers of Francis Durbridge, police procedurals like *Dixon of Dock Green* and *Z-Cars*, the musical offerings of Val Doonican and the Black and White Minstrels, and the comic capers of Ken Dodd and Mike Yarwood.

Television was to be one of several gadgets which enhanced the Murphys' lifestyle in the post-war years. By the start of the 1950s they were well settled in their home at one end of the Forge Cottage. Although the cottage was supplied with mains water and electricity, it lacked a damp course, fixed bath and sanitation. Walter had lived with such a regime all his life and continued to accept it with equanimity. What did interest him was the host of domestic appliances that were now appearing on the market. He soon had the old kitchen range removed from the living room and replaced with a stove while, over time, the scullery came to be fitted out with a cooker, copper, water heater, washing machine, spin drier and refrigerator.

The land behind the cottage was shared in a quite intricate manner between Walter and his cousin (and landlord) Alan Padwick. The vegetable garden to the

Above – The village green at Preston Candover in the early 1960s. The green had looked quite scruffy between the wars, but in the 1950s its appearance was greatly enhanced when the Parish Council had it turfed and enclosed with decorative posts and chains. Walter made the chains. (110) Right – Walter and Laurie, together with Fred and Laurie Sheail, at the wedding of their niece Esme Smith to Bill Gardner at Brown Candover in 1966. (111)

The Andreae Family

The Andreaes were of German origin and formed part of the banking, trading and land-owning elite of southern Germany. From amongst their number emerged John Charles Andreae, known as "Carlo", who was placed in the firm Nestlé Andreae & Co., traders in dye goods financing, based in London.

Carlo arrived in London in 1870 and joined the community of German bankers and merchants who dwelt in the affluent suburb of Camberwell. He was related to one of these families, that of Alexander Friedrich Kleinwort who in the mid-1850s, after working for some years as a sugar trader in Cuba, had set himself up in London as a merchant banker. His family comprised two sons and two daughters. The sons went into the bank which in 1883 was reformed as Kleinwort Sons & Co. Alexander died in 1886.

The Kleinwort office was small and many of its staff were family relatives. These came to include, for a time, Carlo Andreae who married Alexander's daughter Sophie in 1873. They had six children, of whom four were boys.

Carlo died of pneumonia in 1888, after which the children's uncle, young Alexander Kleinwort, stepped in as surrogate father. He formed a particularly strong bond with the second son, Herman Anton. Born in 1876, Herman had a flair for languages and was an accomplished sportsman and equestrian. After attending Dulwich College, he was sent abroad to further his education at institutions in Karlsruhe and Antwerp. He then joined Kleinworts as an apprentice banker in 1897.

In 1900 he was sent off on a tour of the bank's international correspondents, during which time he found himself caught up in the Boxer Rebellion. On rejoining Kleinworts, he quickly proved his worth and was promoted to manager status in 1904. In that same year he married a businessman's daughter, Christiana Candida Ahrens. They were to have three daughters and two sons.

Herman became increasingly involved in making strategic decisions on the bank's business and thus in 1907 he was invited to become a junior partner. In due course he became a senior partner and occupied a dominating position in the bank. His exploits as a yachtsman, athlete, huntsman and skier were also frequently reported in the press.

His first marriage ended in divorce and in 1934 he married Joy Amelia Nitch-Smith. A year later he purchased Moundsmere Manor at

Herman Anton Andreae and Christiana Ahrens on their engagement in 1904. (112)

Preston Candover. This allowed him to pursue fully his hunting interest. In 1945 he took over as Master of the Hampshire Hunt and continued in the post for the next eight years.

During the late 1930s Herman expanded his holding through the purchase of the Down Farm and Wield Manor Farm. He then purchased Lower Farm, Bradley in the early 1940s. The family lived at Wield Manor during the war years while Moundsmere Manor was used as a military hospital. After the war Herman sold Wield Manor to Admiral Sir John Inglis. In the post-war period, under the name Andreae Estates Ltd, the farms were moulded into a substantial enterprise with grain production handled at Moundsmere and the Down Farm, dairying at Moundsmere, and pig farming at Bradley.

With the onset of the Blitz, Herman retired to his country estate, though he did later agree to return as a general supervisor of the bank's affairs. In 1947, when Kleinworts was converted from a partnership into a limited company, he was appointed a Director. He finally retired from the bank in 1961 and died four years later.

Joy was an active member of the local community, serving as President of both the WI and the local Conservative Association. In his last years Herman had a dower house built at Moundsmere which, together with some 170 acres of land, was bequeathed to Joy in his will. She moved into the house following Herman's death but did not live there for long, retiring to a nursing home where she died in 1977.

Of Herman's two sons, the younger, Peter, died from tuberculosis in 1932. The other son, Herman K. – known as "Sonny" – joined the bank in 1936 and was still serving as a Director when he died in 1971. He was married during the war and had five children.

His son Mark attended Lincoln College, Oxford. After a spell at the bank, he decided to make a career as a professional farmer and took over the management of the Moundsmere Estate after his grandfather's death.

The Preston Candover Parish Council in 1951. The occasion was the presentation of the BEM to Mrs Fanny Thorne for 50 years' work on the land. Walter stands second from the right. The other Council members were (from left) Reg Whitworth (builder), George Westbrook (farmer), Elizabeth Aris (owner of Preston Manor Farm), Mrs Daisy Cosier (Chairman) and Charles Elbourne (manager of Preston Manor Farm). Daisy Cosier was the daughter of John Thorp, the butcher. She served as a teacher at the school and was at one time Headmistress. (113)

rear of the cottage belonged to Alan, while Walter had a piece of ground up in the meadow behind the smithy which his uncle had first let him use for a vegetable plot back in the 1920s. Alan and Walter also rented plots on the nearby Parish allotments. They each owned a variety of sheds and garages up in the meadow and shared the access to them. The meadow itself had been used at various times as an orchard, as grazing for a pony, and for keeping pigs, goats, chickens and the odd duck. Walter continued to keep a pig till 1950 and poultry till the late 1960s. At one time he also went in for rearing ferrets. He could sometimes be very soft hearted towards the wildlife that inhabited the meadow – he made do without his hayrake one year because some house martins had made a nest on it in the shed. Nonetheless he always kept a shotgun handy for any rabbit or pigeon that dared stray into his vegetable garden.

Walter reached his 50th birthday in November 1950 and over the following years he came to assume his place as a local "character". Known universally as "Murph", he became enormously popular throughout the district. He was not a church-goer but he did take an active part in most village activities, whether this was organising the bonfire at the Guy Fawkes Night party or filling balloons with hydrogen at the summer fete. He joined the Parish Council in 1950 and served as Chairman from 1964-69, while Alan served as Parish Clerk. He took over the Padwicks' membership of the Farriers' Association and became

Walter outside the pigsty in the meadow behind the smithy, together with his grandson Philip and the family pig, 1950. This was the last pig to be reared in the meadow. (114)

Secretary of the Winchester Branch in 1950, serving in that capacity for some 20 years. Also, from 1966-69 he ran an evening class in metalwork at a school in Alresford.

*

Several of the landowners of the pre-war years were still present in the Candover Valley in the 1950s. Colonel Courage remained at Preston House till his death in 1961, after which the estate was bought by Colonel Vincent Paravicini, the son of a former Swiss Ambassador to the Court of St James'. During the 1940s Herman Andreae acquired additional land which increased his holding to over 2000 acres. He continued to farm this land throughout the post-war years and it remained in his family's ownership after

*Left – Stenbury Drive, built by the Basingstoke Rural District Council in 1949. (115)
Below – Upper Barn, an isolated keeper's cottage, located about half a mile north of the village, abandoned in the post-war years. The same fate befell Cannon's Down Cottages, the Murphys' first home. (116)*

his death in 1965. Further down the valley the Savill family remained in occupation of Chilton Manor Farm. The Manor Farm at Brown Candover had been acquired in 1943 by Major Charles Ball. During the 1950s he acquired further farms in Northington which he brought together with Manor Farm to form the Brown Candover Estate.

The advent of a new town and country planning regime in the post-war years led to the Candover Valley being classified in the County Development Plan as an area of "great landscape value" where the emphasis would be on restricting development. Nonetheless, Preston Candover was to see significant development during the 1950s and '60s.

Improvements to the standard of living were gradually achieved following the installation of electric power in 1939 and piped water in 1947. Community facilities were enhanced with the opening of a new village hall in the mid-1950s. The village school became a primary school in 1948 and thereafter the older children were sent to Perrin's School at Alresford. The existing school buildings at Preston were replaced in 1965. New cottages were built for farm workers. A small Council estate called Stenbury Drive was built in 1949 while a further six bungalows for pensioners were later built at Axford.

By far the greatest pressure for change came from those middle class professionals who were now able to live in the country and commute each day to Basingstoke, Winchester and increasingly to London. Some of the old cottages within the village were redeveloped while new houses were built on the former paddocks and gardens. Preston thus increased in size from around 50 dwellings in 1945 to over 70 in 1966, while Axford grew from a hamlet of nine cottages into a settlement of some 20 houses and bungalows.

During the interwar years the population of Preston and Nutley had declined from 538 in 1911 to 480 in 1931 and, despite the increase in housing, the figure remained at about this level during the post-war period. There was, however, a marked increase in the number of parishioners who were middle aged or elderly. In 1966 those people aged between 20-39 comprised 16% of the population, compared to 31% in 1901. Those aged over 60 in 1966 comprised 28%, compared to 11% in 1901.

A major consequence of the war had been the introduction of daily commuting into village life. This had not really been an option in the interwar years, owing to the lack of suitable public transport, even though by the late 1930s Basingstoke had grown into a commercial and industrial centre of some significance. Its industries included agricultural engineering and the manufacture of motor vehicles, leather goods, aeronautical instruments, clothing and pharmaceuticals. During the war these firms had contributed a great deal towards the war effort and, in

South Hall cottage in the early 1960s. It had previously been divided in two and occupied by labourers' families. Such property became much sought after by middle class professionals in the prosperous post-war years. For a time in the late 1970s it went by the name of "Tiggywinkle Cottage". (117)

Above – The petrol service station and motor repair garage at Preston Candover in the 1950s. (118)
Right – The new school at Preston Candover which replaced the former school buildings in 1965. The school covered Preston, Nutley, Bradley, Candovers and Northington, and at that time catered for some 80 children. (119)

doing so, had generated an unprecedented demand for labour. To help meet this demand, early morning bus services were laid on to the local villages. One of these passed through Preston at 7.00am.

The numbers joining the daily exodus to work in Basingstoke continued to grow during the 1950s, as the existing industries expanded and new ones were established. In 1962 plans were published for Basingstoke to be expanded to cater for London overspill. The scheme involved the construction of a new shopping area and road system, 8000 new houses and new industrial and commercial development. The town would be served by a new motorway, the M3, which would pass just south of the built-up area. All this created yet more job opportunities for people living in the surrounding countryside.

Thus by the mid-1960s 38% of the working population in Preston and Nutley worked outside the parish. Farming accounted for 28% and no longer had any need for seasonal labour. The two general stores, the two pubs and the motor repair garage continued in business throughout the 1950s and '60s. The carpenter closed down in 1944, but the blacksmith and Whitworths the builders continued to operate. There was also Fred Earwicker who set up in business in

Above – The new village hall which replaced the former converted army hut in the mid-1950s. (120)
Left – One of Preston's two general stores in 1966. The shop was for many years run by the Light family, during which time it also contained the Post Office. In 1935 Mrs Light sold the business to Percy Osgood who had previously had a shop at Ropley. The Osgoods kept the store going for the next 30 years and added an extension in 1960. (121)

The Courage Family

Lieutenant-Colonel Miles Rafe Ferguson Courage belonged to a large and illustrious family who owned one of the leading brewery companies in the country. The brewery had been founded at Horsleydown in Southwark in 1787 by John Courage. John was descended from a French Huguenot family who had settled in Scotland in the 1670s. He had come down to London in 1779 to act as agent for Scottish interests along the Thames. The brewery expanded rapidly and eventually became the family's sole business interest. It passed to his son John who brought his own sons into the company as partners. The family partnership continued until 1888 when the firm was made into a limited company called Courage & Co.

John's third son Edward was made a partner in 1854. He then served as chairman of the company from 1893 till his death in 1904. He married a ship owner's daughter, Helen Rosa Marshall, in 1860 and settled at Shenfield Place in Brentwood, Essex where they raised a family of eight girls and three boys, one of whom was Miles, born in 1872.

Miles chose to pursue a military career, during the course of which he met Kathleen Roma Beatty. She was the daughter of Captain David Longfield Beatty of Borrowdale, County Wexford. Her brother later became famous as Admiral Sir David Beatty. Miles and Kathleen were married in 1899. Shortly afterwards he saw service in South Africa. During the First World War he served with the Royal Field Artillery on the Western Front and was appointed Lieutenant-Colonel in 1915. He was later wounded and awarded the DSO before being demobilised in Belgium in 1919.

Alongside his military career Miles played his part in the running of Courage & Co. He was made a Director in 1905 and spent much of his working life managing the Courage brewery at Alton and the public houses attached to it. These were the first premises to be bought by the company outside Southwark, and were acquired so that they could have a site where the water was suitable for the brewing of pale ale. In the 1920s they acquired the Farnham United Breweries and consolidated the whole business at Alton.

For a time Miles and Kathleen lived at Sutton Manor, Sutton Scotney. They also owned a considerable estate in Perthshire. Then in 1933 they purchased the Preston House Estate at Preston Candover. At first the estate comprised just the West and East Park and Home Farm. A couple of years later Miles purchased Nutley

Lieutenant-Colonel Miles Courage (122)

Manor Farm from Edward Kenward. He also bought Flockmoor Farm at Axford from the Kimber family and subsequently created a new farm called Poasley, made up of land formerly within the holdings of the Nutley Manor and Flockmoor Farms. During the 1940s he held Poasley Farm in hand and did the same at Nutley Manor Farm in the 1950s.

A keen sportsman, Miles kept a stable of hunters at Preston House. He was Joint Master of the Hampshire Hunt from 1937-39 and Master from 1939-44. For many years he served on the Basingstoke RDC and in 1930 was made Sheriff of Hampshire. He and Kathleen also played an active part in village life. They gave a Christmas party every year with performances from the Dummer Mummers. In the mid-1950s he provided the ground for the building of a new village hall and was very supportive of the village tennis club.

Preston House was fully staffed until the outbreak of the Second World War. Thereafter Miles and Kathleen had to manage on their own, with the help of two dailies. Kathleen died in 1949. Miles subsequently married an old friend, Ingrid Burton, and continued to live quietly on the estate while the house gradually fell into disrepair around him. He died at Preston House in 1961.

Miles and Kathleen had three sons. The second son, Maurice Vandeleur, went into Courage & Co. and was made responsible for the general management of the public houses. The eldest son, Rafe, entered the Royal Navy in 1916. During the Second World War he commanded a destroyer, HMS *Havock*, at Narvik and in various other operations. Later he lived at the Old Rectory at Bradley where he died in 1960.

Left – One of the permanent milking bails at Moth Farm, Brown Candover. Walter made the fittings, railings and gates. (143)
Below – The yard at Preston Manor Farm. In the early 1950s the old barn at the rear was adapted to accommodate winnowing and grain drying machinery. The galvanised extension in the foreground contained storage bins. Walter supplied various fittings, including grills for the grain drier and the ladders and catwalk supports for the storage bins. (144)

income from construction-related work. Some of this work came from Preston's tradesmen and also from a number of building contractors engaged on projects in the district. The latter were especially evident in the 1960s when Colonel Paravicini had major restoration work carried out at Preston House and the Jervoise family had the mansion at Herriard Park rebuilt.

Much of work, however, stemmed from improvements to farmsteads, in particular from the installation of grain driers and silos, especially in the early 1950s, and from the construction of pens for cattle and pigs. Walter was particularly involved where farmers had driers and corn bins installed in existing barns, for then they would need customised fittings for ladders and catwalks. He was also closely involved in providing stanchions, grills and gates for the milking bails on the Paterson holdings at Hatch Warren and Moth Farm. A particular feature of this work was the use of tubular metal to construct gates, posts and gratings.

All these developments, of course, took place at a time of considerable optimism in British farming. By the end of the 1960s doubts had begun to emerge as to whether this optimism was fully justified. Concerns were now being expressed about the ethics of "factory farming", the loss of landscape quality, the ecological effects of herbicides and pesticides. For the moment, however, in areas such as the Candover Valley the farmers remained generally prosperous and continued to invest in and improve their properties. And for those people who provided a service to the farming community – people such as the local blacksmith – it was a very agreeable time.

Preston House in 1966, following restoration work undertaken for Colonel Paravicini. (145)

Walter outside the smithy in 1959, holding up a "bone shaker" bicycle. Seated on the bicycle is Colin Cosier. Colin had come to live in Preston Candover in the late 1930s, after a lifetime spent working in the furniture, motor and aircraft industries in England and Canada. He set up a workshop behind his house and there he turned out very fine pieces of carpentry to order. Thus when G. Turnor & Son, cycle dealers of Alresford, wanted the bone shaker's wheels restored, they engaged Colin to deal with the woodwork and Walter to fashion new iron tyres. (146)

The '70s & Beyond

In the post-war years, whenever the family gathered at the Forge Cottage on a Sunday afternoon, Walter would invariably dress up for the occasion in his best shirt, tie and suit, and then put on a pair of highly polished black boots. The boots were a matter of some puzzlement to his grandsons for, having put them on, he would then just sit in the armchair chatting. For him, of course, it was a ritual he had grown up with and he was left highly bewildered one day in the early 1970s when he went into Alresford to buy a new pair of best Sunday boots and was greeted with total incomprehension.

It was just one of many small incidents which revealed to him how habits and customs were changing in ways he did not altogether care for. Over the post-war years he had looked with disquiet on the nation's declining moral standards, its strike-prone docks and car factories and, most of all, its revolting teenagers, with their noisy music, their weird clothes and hairstyles, and their roving gangs of Teddy Boys and Mods and Rockers. His views on such things were derived mainly from the columns of the *Daily Express* and the *News of the World*, with a more local slant provided by the *Hants & Berks Gazette* and the gossip picked up from friends and customers. From such gossip he came to look upon Basingstoke as the prime sink of depravity in the district and was very disturbed when its delinquent ways impinged on the village, such as when motorcycle gangs came out and broke up dances at the hall.

The revolution in the nation's eating habits also left him somewhat bemused. During the 1950s the village stores acquired freezers and so Walter and Laurie were able to indulge in such novelties as fish fingers and arctic roll. Nonetheless, he really disliked the whole culture of tinned and packaged foods, the blandness of post-war cheese and sausages, and all the strange new foreign fruits and cuisine that appeared during these years. He was out on a job one day in the 1970s when the lady of the house gave him an aubergine fresh from her greenhouse, and he and Laurie were left deeply puzzled as to what they were supposed to do with it. Walter himself generally stuck with what he had always known – Shredded Wheat for breakfast, Rich Tea or Digestive biscuits for elevensies, bread and fruit cake for tea, with perhaps a tin of salmon or some watercress fresh from the beds at Alresford on Saturdays. The centrepiece of Sunday dinner was always a roast joint. Weekday meals would comprise the remains of the joint, eaten cold or minced, a steak and kidney pie perhaps, or a rasher pudding or fried fish. Yoghurt made no impact whatsoever on his diet. His dessert was always some heavy jam roly-poly, queen's pudding, spotted dick, or suet pudding thick with treacle.

Above – The Preston Candover Over-Sixties Club, photographed in the park beside the village hall in the early 1970s. Walter stands in the back row 7th from the left. Laurie sits just in front of him. Other people include: back row, far left Fred Earwicker; far right Alan Padwick, with Flo' sitting on Laurie's left. **(147)**
Right – Walter and Laurie at Haslemere in Surrey at the wedding of their grandson Philip in October 1975. **(148)**

In 1970 Walter finally started to draw his State Pension, though he gave no thought to retirement and for a while life carried on much as before. Soon, however, he came to appreciate that, with his and Laurie's pensions amounting in total to some £2000 a year, he was now better off than he had ever been in his life. Thus, very gradually, the business became more akin to a hobby. Sometimes he might be asked to fashion a garden gate, fire screen or flowerpot stand, and during the 1970s he much enjoyed dabbling in the ornamental side of his craft. But more often the work comprised little more than a collection of odd jobs like sharpening an axe or mending a spring for an up-and-over garage door.

By the late 1960s, as one of the few traditional blacksmiths still in business, Walter found himself the object of considerable interest. He was "discovered" by the local media in June 1968 when he opened the village fete by reviving the tradition of firing the anvil. The *Southern Evening Echo* subsequently interviewed him for a full page feature on his life and times. Then Southern Television sent out a camera crew to film a piece for their regional news roundup. In the 1970s he took up several invitations to demonstrate his craft at steam rallies and heavy horse shows.

As the pressure of work lessened, so Walter's over-riding interest became focused on his garden and allotment. He joined with others in forming a Gardening Club, served as its President, and subsequently received the Royal Horticultural Society's Banksian Medal in recognition of his services. His health during these years was reasonably good, except for growing deafness which gradually caused him to withdraw from many social activities. In these years too his grandsons married and great-grandchildren came on the scene, giving him a new generation of toddlers to show round the smithy.

If he ever thought about how he might depart this life, Walter would probably have preferred to go while working in the smithy – to have had, say, a

*Right – Walter deep in discussion with a local reporter after having fired the anvil at the village fete on 8 June 1968. **(149)***
Far right – A selection of clippings from the local press.

75

Left – Walter making a horseshoe at the Chilcomb Steam Fair in 1978. (150) Above – Walter, as President of the Gardening Club, overseeing the planting of a tree outside the village hall to commemorate the Silver Jubilee of 1977. (151)

seizure while hammering away at the anvil and then to have had a grand funeral at St Mary's, the church packed to the doors with all his customers, friends and fellow blacksmiths. But the years went by and he continued to potter along while his contemporaries died or retired and moved away.

By the late 1970s the business was bringing in about £700 a year but, with costs continually rising, the profits soon dwindled and in 1978 it finally registered a loss. Even so, Walter shrank from taking the irrevocable step of actually closing it down. He had always regretted that he did not have a son to whom he could pass it on. Whether a son would have wanted the business – and whether he would have found it possible to work with his father – was something Walter never seemed to consider. For some years after his grandsons were born, he nursed the notion that one of them might some day join him at the smithy, even though neither of them showed any aptitude for craft work and even if they had, their mother had very different ideas for their future. Over the years they progressed through grammar school to university and on to careers in the professions. The whole business of "Eleven-Plus" and "O-Levels" and "A-Levels" and "Finals" rather passed Walter by. Nonetheless it did become apparent to him that, when the day came to give up the smithy, there would be no-one within the family to take it over.

The crunch point finally came in the early 1980s. By then it was clear he could no longer cope, mentally or physically, with the work or with running the business, and he reluctantly agreed to close it down. In 1983, accompanied by his daughter Laurie, Walter travelled in to Winchester to the offices of his auditor and there the formalities were carried out, the proceedings going completely over his head. And so, after who knows how many centuries, the Preston Candover smithy was finally laid to rest.

It was to be one of several major changes which impacted on the Murphys' long established lifestyle. In the 1970s Walter's cousin and landlord, Alan Padwick, had sold the top half of the meadow behind the smithy for the erection of six Council bungalows. At around the same time the former grocer's shop and bakehouse on the next door property were demolished and a neo-Georgian house built on the site. It came to be occupied by the Drew family – Mr John Drew, a veterinary surgeon, and his wife Doctor Bridget Drew, a research scientist with ADAS. Alan Padwick died in 1981, his widow the following year. Their daughter subsequently put the whole property up for sale and it was acquired by the Drews.

The Murphys continued to live on as tenants at their end of the Forge Cottage, but they became increasingly dependent on family and neighbours for their shopping needs and for sorting out their financial affairs. Since the late 1960s Laurie had suffered greatly with arthritis. Two hip replacements in the 1970s had given her a welcome respite, but now she was becoming increasingly disabled. She had never entertained any sentimental notions about country cottages and would have happily moved years before

Walter, together with Jacqueline Savill, during a visit to Chilton Manor in the 1970s to trim the donkeys' feet. (152)

The Murphys' great-grandchildren in the late 1970s. Right – Karen and Andrew Sheail. (153) Far right – Christopher Sheail. (154)

into one of the bungalows in Stenbury Drive. But she knew Walter wanted to stay in his old home and so she never made it an issue. By the early 1980s, however, he had finally come round to the idea, though he insisted they remain in Preston Candover, so it was not till the end of 1985 that one of the bungalows at the top of the meadow became available.

They moved into their new home the following January but by then it was all far too late. For some time it had been apparent that Walter was suffering from the onset of senile dementia. Not only had he found it increasingly difficult to deal with bills and letters, but he also began calling things by the wrong name and, though he could recall past events with perfect clarity, his short term memory deserted him completely. By the Christmas of 1985 his conversation was quite incomprehensible. Finally in April 1986 matters had deteriorated to such an extent that he had to be committed to the Psychiatric Hospital at Basingstoke. Laurie had declined in parallel with him and, after brief spells in various care homes, she too was placed in the Basingstoke hospital.

Walter soon lost all power of speech and ceased to recognise anyone, even Laurie when she was wheeled round to see him. But he was now free from the stress of coping with everyday life and was treated with great kindness by the staff, and as a result his health blossomed, giving him the complexion of a rosy apple and the strength of an ox. And so he lived there quite contentedly until early in May 1989 when he suffered a major stroke. He died a few days later on 8 May 1989 at the age of 88.

He was cremated at the Aldershot Crematorium. Then a few weeks later on a glorious morning in June, a memorial service was held for him at St Mary's in Preston Candover, after which his ashes were interred in the Garden of Remembrance in the churchyard. To the majority of parishioners, of course, his passing meant very little, so the service was attended by a fairly small congregation - about 30 former customers and neighbours and their children. Laurie remained a patient at the Basingstoke Hospital for a couple more years until she died in September 1991, just after her 91st birthday. Her ashes were buried next to Walter's in the churchyard at Preston Candover.

Walter in 1986 after being committed to the Basingstoke Psychiatric Hospital, photographed on an outing to an animal sanctuary near Andover. (155)

Once vacated, the Forge Cottage was sold off and extensively refurbished. The land behind the former smithy was merged with the adjoining property and used by the Drews in pursuit of their equine interests which included racing and dressage. The old galvanised iron sheds and derelict pig sties were all swept away and replaced by a series of stable blocks, grouped around a concrete yard. The smithy, however, was retained, used first as a workshop, then converted into a one-bedroom bungalow for the stable girl.

Thus the Preston Candover smithy finally met the fate of its contemporaries, with a nameplate – in this case *The Old Blacksmith's Shop* – as the only reminder of the bustling country craft that was carried on at this spot for so many years.

THE FORTUNES OF THE PRESTON CANDOVER SMITHY 1910-14/1926-70

The prime source of information about the Preston Candover smithy during the 20th century is a set of ledgers, containing the accounts of individual customers. The ledger for the years between 1915 and the spring of 1925 is missing. Otherwise there is a complete record for the years 1910-14 and 1926-83 when the business closed down. However, once Walter Murphy started drawing his State Pension in 1970, the business became more akin to a hobby than a strictly commercial undertaking, and thus it ceased to reflect contemporary social and economic trends. The graphs therefore only show the fortunes of the smithy up to 1970.

In order to take account of inflation over the period, Graphs 1-3 show annual income at 1970 prices.

1. ANNUAL INCOME

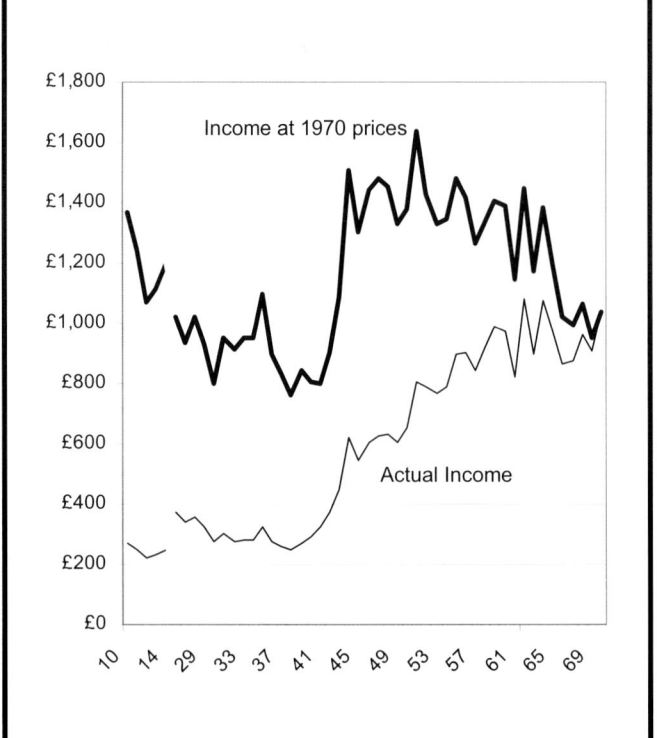

2. ANNUAL INCOME BY LOCATION OF CUSTOMER'S PROPERTY

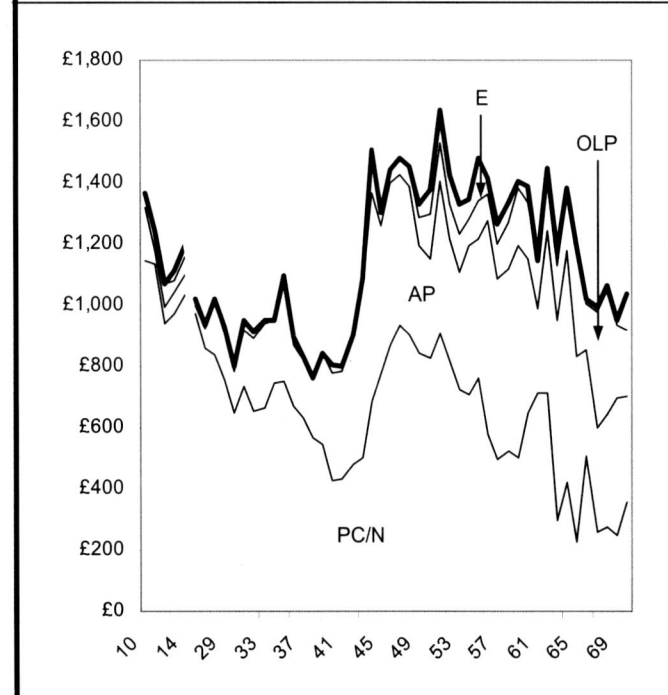

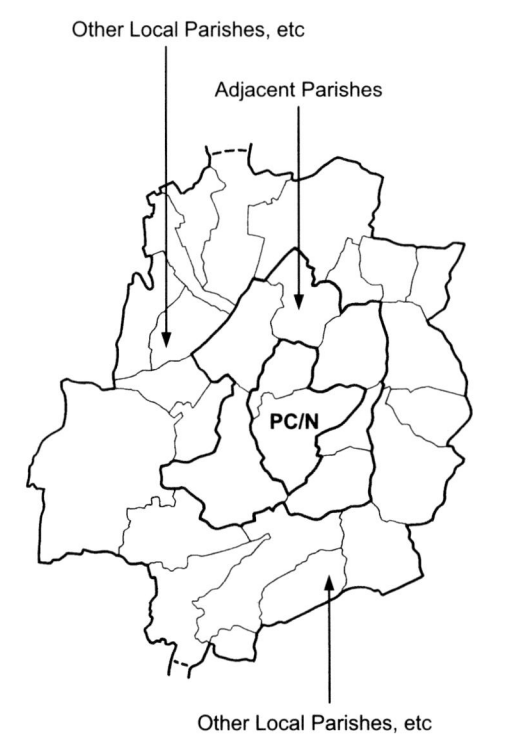

PC/N: Preston Candover and Nutley
AP: Adjacent Parishes
OLP: Other Local Parishes, etc*
E: Elsewhere

* All the local authority areas shown were civil parishes, except for Basingstoke which was a municipal borough. For the names of the areas, see map on page 3.

3. ANNUAL INCOME BY TYPE OF WORK

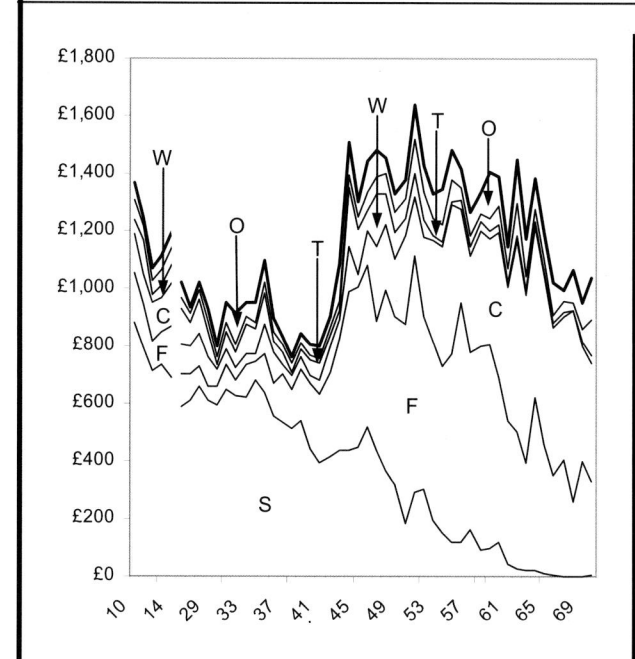

S: Shoeing
F: Farm Implements, Carts & Machinery
C: Construction-Related Work
W: Wheelbinding
T: Tools
O: Other

4. ANNUAL CONSUMPTION OF OXYGEN & ACETYLENE GAS 1931-46

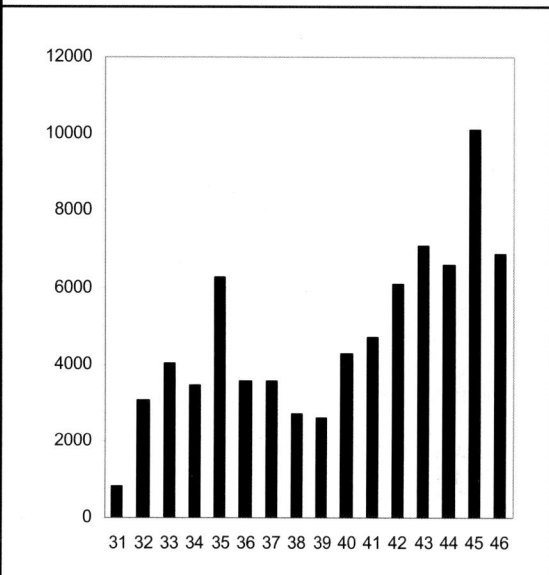

Consumption of oxygen & acetylene rendered in cubic feet.

5. NUMBER OF HORSES SHOD ANNUALLY

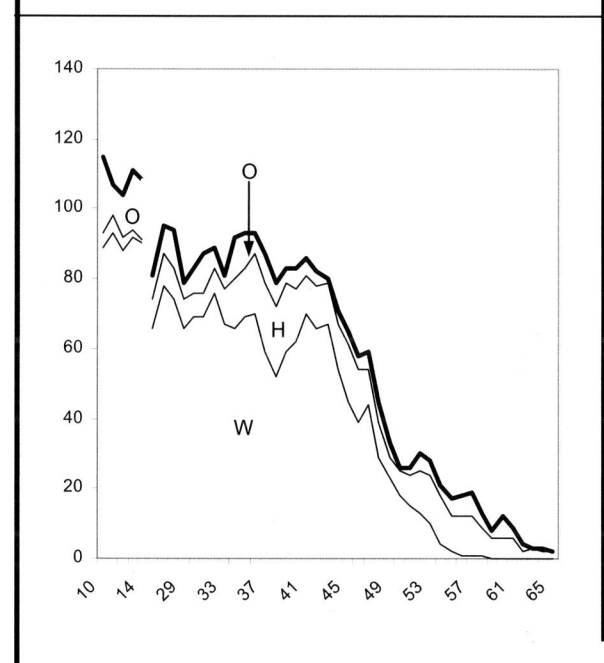

6. NUMBER OF HORSESHOES MADE & FITTED ANNUALLY

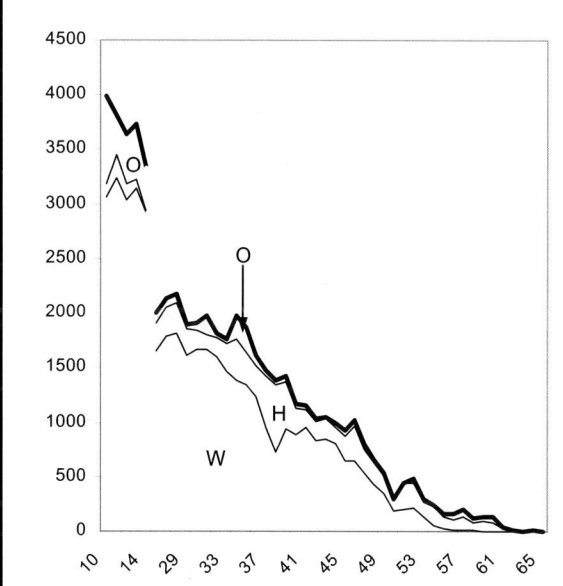

W: Workhorses belonging to farmers & tradesmen
H: Hunters
O: Other

Bibliography

PRIMARY SOURCES

ORAL
Interviews held with Walter Murphy and other members of his family during the late 1960s, and more recent interviews held with family descendants or friends of the principal customers of the Preston Candover smithy during the period 1910-70.

MANUSCRIPT
These mainly comprise the business papers of the Preston Candover smithy: the record of work undertaken for customers 1910-14/1926-70; Day Books 1945-70; Auditor's Reports 1950-83; British Oxygen Co. Invoices 1931-65; sundry invoices, receipts and correspondence. Information was also drawn from an undergraduate dissertation, compiled by Philip Sheail in 1966-7, which contained the findings of a population census and other details pertaining to Preston Candover and Nutley in 1966.

PRINTED
This mainly comprises information obtained from local newspapers, the *Hampshire Chronicle* and the *Hants & Berks Gazette*, and also from the Preston Candover parish magazine *Oxdrove* which was first published in 1966. These sources were particularly useful for obtaining biographical details about the blacksmith's customers.

Front Cover:
Looking south-east from Tull's Hill over Manor Farm, the old St Mary's churchyard, and Lower Farm at Preston Candover.

Back Cover:
Looking north over Manor Farm and Candover Park at Brown Candover.

Both photographs taken in the mid-1960s.

SECONDARY SOURCES
There is an enormous literature on the changing face of the countryside, the nature and demise of rural crafts, and farm mechanisation. The books listed here are mainly confined to those which contain specific information about the Candover Valley or individual people, and those which provide a contemporary insight into the blacksmith's craft.

Arnold, J. 1968 *The Shell Book of Country Crafts*
Bailey, J. 1994 *The Village Blacksmith*, Princes Risborough
Brown, R. 1994 *Basingstoke – A Pictorial History 1935-1965*, Chichester
Evans, D. (Editor) [c1990] *The War Years – A collection of personal memories from residents in the Candover Valley*, Preston Candover
Fox, L.M. 1928 *Handbook for Oxy-Acetylene Welders*
Grimshaw, A. 1982 *The Horse: A Bibliography of British Books 1851-1976*
Holmes, C.M 1928 *The Principles and Practice of Horse-Shoeing*, Leeds
Hughes, A. 1991 *The Close Brewery, Hadlow*, Tonbridge
Hunting, W. 1895 *The Art of Horse-Shoeing – A Manual for Farriers*
Jebb, L. 1991 *Preston House – A History*, Preston Candover
Langdon, R. 1973 "The exploits of the 'Cecil Rhodes of the Pacific' ", *Pambu* (The quarterly newsletter of the Pacific Manuscripts Bureau, Australian National University, Canberra) No. 33
Locke, S. 2000 *George Marston: Shackleton's Antarctic Artist*, Winchester
Mills, O. 1965 *Wield – Parish History*, Wield
Northington Village History Group, 1996 *Northington and Swarraton – 100 Years of Parish History 1890-1990*, Northington
Pudney, J. 1971 *A Draught of Contentment: The Story of the Courage Group*
Roberts, E. 1975 *In and Around Alresford*, Alresford
Roberts, E. 1992 *In and Around Alresford, Volume 2* Alresford
Rolt, L.T.C. 1969 *Waterloo Ironworks – A History of Taskers of Andover, 1809-1968*, Newton Abbot
Rural Industries Bureau [c1950] *Oxy-Acetylene Welding for Country Smiths*
Rural Industries Bureau 1955 *The Blacksmith's Craft*
Sheail, P. 1979 *A Downland Village – Portrait of a Hampshire Parish*, Winchester
Sheail, P. 2003 *Wilfred Buckley of Moundsmere and the Clean Milk Campaign*, Winchester
Sturt, G. 1923 *The Wheelwright's Shop*, Cambridge
Tibbenham, L. (Editor) [c.1920] *Practical Handbook on Oxy-Acetylene Welding*
Wake, J. 1997 *Kleinwort Benson: The history of two families in banking*, Oxford
Wake, J. 2000 *Beyond the Banking Hall – A History of the Kleinwort Family*, Stroud
Webber, R. 1971 *The Village Blacksmith*, Newton Abbot
Whitlock, R. 1988 *The Lost Village – Rural Life between the Wars*
Ziegler, P. 1988 *The Sixth Great Power – Barings 1762-1929*